THE MIDE'WIWIN OR "GRAND MEDICINE SOCIETY" OF THE OJIBWA • HOFFMAN, WALTER JAMES

Publisher's Note

Purchase of this book entitles you to a free trial membership in the publisher's book club at www.rarebooksclub.com. (Time limited offer.) Simply enter the barcode number from the back cover onto the membership form on our home page. The book club entitles you to select from millions of books at no additional charge. You can also download a digital copy of this and related books to read on the go. Simply enter the title or subject onto the search form to find them.

Note: This is an historic book. Pages numbers, where present in the text, refer to the first edition of the book and may also be in indexes.

If you have any questions, could you please be so kind as to consult our Frequently Asked Questions page at www.rarebooksclub.com/faqs.cfm? You are also welcome to contact us there.
Publisher: General Books LLC™, Memphis, TN, USA, 2012. ISBN: 9781153711807.
Proofreading: pgdp.net

❋ ❋ ❋ ❋ ❋ ❋ ❋ ❋

CONTENTS.

	Page
Introduction 2	149
Shamans 6	156
Midē´wiwin 10	164
Midē´wigân 21	187
First degree 22	189
Preparatory instruction 22	189
Midē´ therapeutics 25	197
Imploration for clear weather 30	207
Initiation of candidate 31	210
Descriptive notes 36	220
Second degree 37	224
Preparation of candidate 37	224
Initiation of candidate 41	231
Descriptive notes 43	236
Third degree 45	240
Preparation of candidate 45	241
Initiation of candidate 47	243
Descriptive notes 51	251
Fourth degree 53	255
Preparation of candidate 53	257
Initiation of candidate 54	258
Descriptive notes 60	274
Dzhibai´ Midē´wigân 62	278
Initiation by substitution 63	281
Supplementary notes 65	286
Pictography 65	286
Music 66	289
Dress and ornaments 69	298
Future of the society 70	299
Footnotes 70	
Index 0	

Musical Notation:
following Plate X.b .... 30 (pgs. 207-208)
pages 213 33
, 214 33
, 216 34

following Plate XVII.a .... 58 (pgs. 266-273)
pages 285 65
, 286 65
147

ILLUSTRATIONS.

Illustrations have been placed as close as practicable to their discussion in the text. Multi-part Plates have been divided. The printed page numbers show the original location of the illustrations. Plates and Figures were numbered continuously within each Bureau of Ethnology volume, so there is no Plate I in this article.

Plate			Page.
II.	..2	Map showing present distribution of Ojibwa	150
III.	10	Red Lake and Leech Lake records	166
IV.	13	Sikas´sige's record	170
V.	14	Origin of Ânishinâ´bēg	172
VI.	18	Facial decoration	174
VII.	 19	Facial decoration	178
VIII.	 18	Ojibwa's record	182
IX.		Mnemonic songs: IX.a 23	193
		IX.b 24	
		IX.c 25	
X.		Mnemonic songs: X.a 28	202
		X.b 30	
		X.c 31	
		X.d 35	
XI	36	Sacred objects	220
XII.	 39	Invitation sticks	236
XIII.		Mnemonic songs: XIII.a 39	238
		XIII.b 40	
		XIII.c 41	
		XIII.d 44	
XIV.		Mnemonic songs: XIV.a 47	288
		XIV.b 48	
		XIV.c 50	
		XIV.d 52	

XV. 45	Sacred posts		240
XVI.	Mnemonic songs: XVI.a 54		244
	XVI.b 55		
	XVI.c 63		
	XVI.d 64		
XVII.	Mnemonic songs: XVII.a 58		266
	XVII.b 56		
XVIII. 62	Jĕs´sakkĭd´ removing disease		278
XIX. 65	Birch-bark records		286
XX. 66	Sacred bark scroll and contents		288
XXI. 66	Midē´ relics from Leech Lake		390
XXII.	Mnemonic songs: XXII.a 67		392
	XXII.b 68		
XXIII. 70	Midē´ dancing garters		298
Fig. 1. 7	Herbalist preparing medicine and treating patient		159
2. ... 0	Sikas´sigĕ's combined charts, showing descent of Mī´nabō´zho		174
3. . 46	Origin of ginseng		175
4. . 17	Peep-hole post		178
5. . 17	Migration of Ânishinâ´bĕg		179
6. . 20	Birch-bark record, from White Earth		185
7. . 21	Birch-bark record, from Bed Lake		186
8. . 21	Birch-bark record, from Red Lake		186
9. . 21	Eshgibō´ga		187
10. 21	Diagram of Midē´wigân of the first degree		188
11. 22	Interior of Midē´wigân		188
12. 23	Ojibwa drums		190
13. 23	Midē´ rattle		191
14. 23	Midē´ rattle		191
15. 23	Shooting the Mīgis		192
16. 29	Wooden beads		205
17. 29	Wooden effigy		205
18. 29	Wooden effigy		205
19. 36	Hawk-leg fetish		220
20. 37	Hunter's medicine		222
21. 37	Hunter's medicine		222
22. 37	148 Wâbĕnō´ drum		223
23. 37	Diagram of Midē´wigân of the second degree		224
24. 44	Midē´ destroying an enemy		238
25. 45	Diagram of Midē´wigân of the third degree		240
26. 51	Jĕs´sakkân´, or juggler's lodge		252
27. 51	Jĕs´sakkân´, or juggler's lodge		252
28. 51	Jĕs´sakkân´, or juggler's lodge		252
29. 51	Jĕs´sakkân´, or juggler's lodge		252
30. 51	Jĕs´sakkân´, or juggler's lodge		252
31. 52	Jĕs´sakkĭd´ curing woman		255
32. 52	Jĕs´sakkĭd´ curing man		255
33. 53	Diagram of Midē´wigân of the fourth degree		255
34. 53	General view of Midē´wigân		256
35. 62	Indian diagram of ghost lodge		279
36. 69	Leech Lake Midē´ song		295
37. 69	Leech Lake Midē´ song		296
38. 69	Leech Lake Midē´ song		297
39. 69	Leech Lake Midē´ song		297

map thumbnail.
Larger Map 0 — Ojibwa Indian Reservations in Minnesota and Wisconsin. I Red Lake. II White Earth. III Winnibigoshish. IV Cass Lake. V Leech Lake. VI Deer Creek. VII Bois Forte. VIII Vermillion Lake. IX Fond du Lac. X Mille Lacs. XI Lac Court Oreílle. XII La Pointe. XIII Lac de Flanibeau. XIV Red Cliff. XV Grand Portage. 149

THE MIDĒ´WIWIN OR "GRAND MEDICINE SOCIETY" OF THE OJIBWAY.

By W. J. Hoffman.

INTRODUCTION.

The Ojibwa is one of the largest tribes of the United States, and it is scattered over a considerable area, from the Province of Ontario, on the east, to the Red River of the North, on the west, and from Manitoba southward through the States of Minnesota, Wisconsin, and Michigan. This tribe is, strictly speaking, a timber people, and in its westward migration or dispersion has never passed beyond the limit of the timber growth which so remarkably divides the State of Minnesota into two parts possessing distinct physical features. The western portion of this State is a gently undulating prairie which sweeps away to the Rocky Mountains, while the eastern portion is heavily timbered. The dividing line, at or near the meridian of 95° 50' west longitude, extends due north and south, and at a point about 75 miles south of the northern boundary the timber line trends toward the northwest, crossing the State line, 49° north latitude, at about 97° 10' west longitude.

Minnesota contains many thousand lakes of various sizes, some of which are connected by fine water courses, while others are entirely isolated. The wooded country is undulating, the elevated portions being covered chiefly with pine, fir, spruce, and other coniferous trees, and the lowest depressions being occupied by lakes, ponds, or marshes, around which occur the tamarack, willow, and other trees which thrive in moist ground, while the regions between these extremes are covered with oak, poplar, ash, birch, maple, and many other varieties of trees and shrubs.

Wild fowl, game, and fish are still abundant, and until recently have furnished to the Indians the chief source of subsistence.

Tribal organization according to the totemic system is practically broken up, as the Indians are generally located upon or near the several reservations set apart for them by the General Government, where they have been under more or less restraint by the United States Indian agents and the missionaries. Representatives of various totems or gentes may therefore be found upon a single reservation, 150 where they continue to adhere to traditional customs and beliefs, thus presenting an interesting field for ethnologic research.

The present distribution of the Ojibwa in Minnesota and Wisconsin is indicated upon the accompanying map, Pl. II 2
. In the southern portion many of these people have adopted civilized pursuits, but throughout the northern and northwestern part many bands continue to adhere to their primitive methods and are commonly designated "wild Indians." The habitations of many of the latter are rude and primitive. The bands on the northeast shore of Red Lake, as well as a few others farther east, have occupied these isolated sites for an uninterrupted period of about three centuries, as is affirmed by the chief men of the several villages and corroborated by other traditional evidence.

Father Claude Allouëz, upon his arrival in 1666 at Shagawaumikong, or La Pointe, found the Ojibwa preparing to attack the Sioux. The settlement at this point was an extensive one, and in traditions pertaining to the "Grand Medicine Society" frequent allusion is made to the fact that at this place the rites were practiced in their greatest purity.

Mr. Warren, in his History of the Ojibwa Indians,
1 70
bases his belief upon traditional evidence that the Ojibwa first had knowledge of the whites in 1612. Early in the seventeenth century the French missionaries met with various tribes of the Algonkian linguistic stock, as well as with bands or subtribes of the Ojibwa Indians. One of the latter, inhabiting the vicinity of Sault Ste. Marie, is frequently mentioned in the Jesuit Relations as the Saulteurs. This term was applied to all those people who lived at the Falls, but from other statements it is clear that the Ojibwa formed the most important body in that vicinity. La Hontan speaks of the "Outchepoues, alias Sauteurs," as good warriors. The name Saulteur survives at this day and is applied to a division of the tribe.

According to statements made by numerous Ojibwa chiefs of importance the tribe began its westward dispersion from La Pointe and Fond du Lac at least two hundred and fifty years ago, some of the bands penetrating the swampy country of northern Minnesota, while others went westward and southwestward. According to a statement
2 70
of the location of the tribes of Lake Superior, made at Mackinaw in 1736, the Sioux then occupied the southern and northern extremities of that lake. It is possible, however, that the northern bands of the Ojibwa may have penetrated the region adjacent to the Pigeon River and passed west to near their present location, thus avoiding their enemies who occupied the lake shore south of them.

151 From recent investigations among a number of tribes of the Algonkian linguistic division it is found that the traditions and practices pertaining to the Midē′wiwin, Society of the Midē′ or Shamans, popularly designated as the "Grand Medicine Society," prevailed generally, and the rites are still practiced at irregular intervals, though in slightly different forms in various localities.

In the reports of early travelers and missionaries no special mention is made of the Midē′, the Jes′sakkīd′, or the Wâbĕnō′, but the term sorcerer or juggler is generally employed to designate that class of persons who professed the power of prophecy, and who practiced incantation and administered medicinal preparations. Constant reference is made to the opposition of these personages to the introduction of Christianity In the light of recent investigation the cause of this antagonism is seen to lie in the fact that the traditions of Indian genesis and cosmogony and the ritual of initiation into the Society of the Midē′ constitute what is to them a religion, even more powerful and impressive than the Christian religion is to the average civilized man. This opposition still exists among the leading classes of a number of the Algonkian tribes, and especially among the Ojibwa, many bands of whom have been more or less isolated and beyond convenient reach of the Church. The purposes of the society are twofold; first, to preserve the traditions just mentioned, and second, to give a certain class of ambitious men and women sufficient influence through their acknowledged power of exorcism and necromancy to lead a comfortable life at the expense of the credulous. The persons admitted into the society are firmly believed to possess the power of communing with various supernatural beings—manidos—and in order that certain desires may be realized they are sought after and consulted. The purpose of the present paper is to give an account of this society and of the ceremony of initiation as studied and observed at White Earth, Minnesota, in 1889. Before proceeding to this, however, it may be of interest to consider a few statements made by early travelers respecting the "sorcerers or jugglers" and the methods of medication.

In referring to the practices of the Algonkian tribes of the Northwest, La Hontan[3] says:

When they are sick, they only drink Broth, and eat sparingly; and if they have the good luck to fall asleep, they think themselves cur'd: They have told me frequently, that sleeping and sweating would cure the most stubborn Diseases in the World. When they are so weak that they cannot get out of Bed, their Relations come and dance and make merry before 'em, in order to divert 'em. To conclude, when they are ill, they are always visited by a sort of Quacks, (*Jongleurs*); of whom 't will now be proper to subjoin two or three Words by the bye.

A *Jongleur* is a sort of *Physician*, or rather a *Quack*, who being once cur'd of some dangerous Distemper, has the Presumption and Folly to fancy that he is immortal, and possessed of the Power of curing all Diseases, by speaking to the Good and Evil Spirits. Now though every Body rallies upon these Fellows when 152 they are absent, and looks upon 'em as Fools that have lost their Senses by some violent Distemper, yet they allow 'em to visit the Sick; whether it be to divert 'em with their Idle Stories, or to have an Opportunity of seeing them rave, skip about, cry, houl, and make Grimaces and Wry Faces, as if they were possess'd. When all the Bustle is over, they demand a Feast of a Stag and some large Trouts for the Company, who are thus regal'd at once with Diversion and Good Cheer.

When the Quack comes to visit the Patient, he examines him very carefully; *If the Evil Spirit be here*, says he, *we shall quickly dislodge him*. This said, he withdraws by himself to a little Tent made on purpose, where he dances, and sings houling like an Owl; (which gives the Jesuits Occasion to say, *That the Devil converses with 'em*.) After he has made an end of this Quack Jargon, he comes and rubs the Patient in some part of his Body, and pulling some little Bones out of his Mouth, acquaints the Patient, *That these very Bones came out of his Body; that he ought to pluck up a good heart, in regard that his Distemper is but a Trifle; and in fine, that in order to accelerate the Cure, 't will be convenient to send his own and his Relations Slaves to shoot Elks, Deer, &c., to the end they may all eat of that sort of Meat, upon which his Cure does absolutely depend.*

Commonly these Quacks bring 'em some Juices of Plants, which are a sort of Purges, and are called *Maskikik*.

Hennepin, in "A Continuation of the New Discovery," etc.,4 speaks of the religion and sorcerers of the tribes of the St. Lawrence and those living about the Great Lakes as follows:

We have been all too sadly convinced, that almost all the Salvages in general have no notion of a God, and that they are not able to comprehend the most ordinary Arguments on that Subject; others will have a Spirit that commands, say they, in the Air. Some among 'em look upon the Skie as a kind of Divinity; others as an *Otkon* or *Manitou*, either Good or Evil.

These People admit of some sort of Genius in all things; they all believe there is a Master of Life, as they call him, but hereof they make various applications; some of them have a lean Raven, which they carry always along with them, and which they say is the Master of their Life; others have an Owl, and some again a Bone, a Sea-Shell, or some such thing;

There is no Nation among 'em which has not a sort of Juglers or Conjuerers, which some look upon to be Wizards, but in my Opinion there is no Great reason to believe 'em such, or to think that their Practice favours any thing of a Communication with the Devil.

These Impostors cause themselves to be reverenced as Prophets which fore-tell Futurity. They will needs be look'd upon to have an unlimited Power. They boast of being able to make it Wet or Dry; to cause a Calm or a Storm; to render Land Fruitful or Barren; and, in a Word to make Hunters Fortunate or Unfortunate. They also pretend to Physick, and to apply Medicines, but which are such, for the most part as have little Virtue at all in 'em, especially to Cure that Distemper which they pretend to.

It is impossible to imagine, the horrible Howlings and strange Contortions that those Jugglers make of their Bodies, when they are disposing themselves to Conjure, or raise their Enchantments.

Marquette, who visited the Miami, Mascontin and Kickapoo Indians in 1673, after referring to the Indian herbalist, mentions also the ceremony of the "calumet dance," as follows:

They have Physicians amongst them, towards whom they are very liberal when they are sick, thinking that the Operation of the Remedies they take, is proportional to the Presents they make unto those who have prescrib'd them.

153 In connection with this, reference is made by Marquette to a certain class of individuals among the Illinois and Dakota, who were compelled to wear women's clothes, and who were debarred many privileges, but were permitted to "assist at all the Superstitions of their *Juglers*, and their solemn Dances in honor of the *Calumet*, in which they may sing, but it is not lawful for them to dance. They are call'd to their Councils, and nothing is determin'd without their Advice; for, because of their extraordinary way of Living, they are look'd upon as *Manitous*, or at least for great and incomparable Genius's."

That the calumet was brought into requisition upon all occasions of interest is learned from the following statement, in which the same writer declares that it is "the most mysterious thing in the World. The Sceptres of our Kings are not so much respected; for the Savages have such a Deference for this Pipe, that one may call it *The God of Peace and War, and the Arbiter of Life and Death*. Their *Calumet of Peace* is different from the *Calumet of War*; They make use of the former to seal their Alliances and Treaties, to travel with safety, and receive Strangers; and the other is to proclaim War."

This reverence for the calumet is shown by the manner in which it is used at dances, in the ceremony of smoking, etc., indicating a religious devoutness approaching that recently observed among various Algonkian tribes in connection with the ceremonies of the Midē′wiwin. When the calumet dance was held, the Illinois appear to have resorted to the houses in the winter and to the groves in the summer. The above-named authority continues in this connection:

They chuse for that purpose a set Place among Trees, to shelter themselves against the Heat of the Sun, and lay in the middle a large Matt, as a Carpet, to lay upon the God of the Chief of the Company, who gave the Ball; for every one has his peculiar God, whom they call *Manitoa*. It is sometime a Stone, a Bird, a Serpent, or anything else that they dream of in their Sleep; for they think this *Manitoa* will prosper their Wants, as Fishing, Hunting, and other Enterprizes. To the Right of their *Manitoa* they place the *Calumet*, their Great Deity, making round about it a Kind of Trophy with their Arms, viz. their Clubs, Axes, Bows, Quivers, and Arrows. *** Every Body sits down afterwards, round about, as they come, having first of all saluted the *Manitoa*, which they do in blowing the Smoak of their Tobacco upon it, which is as much as offering to it Frankincense. *** This *Preludium* being over, he who is to begin the Dance appears in the middle of the Assembly, and having taken the *Calumet*, presents it to the Sun, as if he wou'd invite him to smoke. Then he moves it into an infinite Number of Postures sometimes laying it near the Ground, then stretching its Wings, as if he wou'd make it fly, and then presents it to the Spectators, who smoke with it one after another, dancing all the while. This is the first Scene of this famous Ball.

The infinite number of postures assumed in offering the pipe appear as significant as the "smoke ceremonies" mentioned in connection with the preparatory instruction of the candidate previous to his initiation into the Midē'wiwin.

154 In his remarks on the religion of the Indians and the practices of the sorcerers, Hennepin says:

As for their Opinion concerning the Earth, they make use of a Name of a certain *Genius*, whom they call *Micaboche*, who has cover'd the whole Earth with water (as they imagine) and relate innumerable fabulous Tales, some of which have a kind of Analogy with the Universal Deluge. These Barbarians believe that there are certain Spirits in the Air, between Heaven and Earth, who have a power to foretell future Events, and others who play the part of Physicians, curing all sorts of Distempers. Upon which account, it happens, that these *Savages* are very Superstitious, and consult their Oracles with a great deal of exactness. One of these Masters-Jugglers who pass for Sorcerers among them, one day caus'd a Hut to be erected with ten thick Stakes, which he fix'd very deep in the Ground, and then made a horrible noise to Consult the Spirits, to know whether abundance of Snow wou'd fall ere long, that they might have good game in the Hunting of Elks and Beavers: Afterward he bawl'd out aloud from the bottom of the Hut, that he saw many Herds of Elks, which were as yet at a very great distance, but that they drew near within seven or eight Leagues of their Huts, which caus'd a great deal of joy among those poor deluded Wretches.

That this statement refers to one or more tribes of the Algonkian linguistic stock is evident, not only because of the reference to the sorcerers and their peculiar methods of procedure, but also that the name of *Micaboche*, an Algonkian divinity, appears. This Spirit, who acted as an intercessor between Ki´tshi Man´idō (Great Spirit) and the Indians, is known among the Ojibwa as Mi´nabō´zho; but to this full reference will be made further on in connection with the Myth of the origin of the Midē´wiwin. The tradition of Nokomis (the earth) and the birth of Manabush (the Mi´nabō´zho of the Menomoni) and his brother, the Wolf, that pertaining to the re-creation of the world, and fragments of other myths, are thrown together and in a mangled form presented by Hennepin in the following words:

Some Salvages which live at the upper end of the River St. *Lawrence*, do relate a pretty diverting Story. They hold almost the same opinion with the former [the Iroquois], that a Woman came down from Heaven, and remained for some while fluttering in the Air, not finding Ground whereupon to put her Foot. But that the Fishes moved with Compassion for her, immediately held a Consultation to deliberate which of them should receive her. The Tortoise very officiously offered its Back on the Surface of the Water. The Woman came to rest upon it, and fixed herself there. Afterwards the Filthiness and Dirt of the Sea gathering together about the Tortoise, there was formed by little and little that vast Tract of Land, which we now call *America*.

They add that this Woman grew weary of her Solitude, wanting some body for to keep her Company, that so she might spend her time more pleasantly. Melancholy and Sadness having seiz'd upon her Spirits, she fell asleep, and a Spirit descended from above, and finding her in that Condition approach'd and knew her unperceptibly. From which Approach she conceived two Children, which came forth out of one of her Ribs. But these two Brothers could never afterwards agree together. One of them was a better Huntsman than the other: they quarreled every day; and their Disputes grew so high at last, that one could not bear with the other. One especially being of a very wild Temper, hated mortally his Brother who was of a milder Constitution, who being no longer able to endure the Pranks of the other, 155 he resolved at last to part from him. He retired then into Heaven, whence, for a Mark of his just Resentment, he causeth at several times his Thunder to rore over the Head of his unfortunate Brother.

Sometime after the Spirit descended again on that Woman, and she conceived a Daughter, from whom (as the Salvages say) were propagated these numerous People, which do occupy now one of the greatest parts of the Universe.

It is evident that the narrator has sufficiently distorted the traditions to make them conform, as much as practicable, to the biblical story of the birth of Christ. No reference whatever is made in the Ojibwa or Menomoni myths to the conception of the Daughter of Nokomis (the earth) by a celestial visitant, but the reference is to one of the wind gods. Mi´nabō´zho became angered with the Ki´tshi Man´idō, and the latter, to appease his discontent, gave to Mi´nabō´zho the rite of the Midēwiwin. The brother of Mi´nabō´zho was destroyed by the malevolent underground spirits and now rules the abode of shadows,—the "Land of the Midnight Sun."

Upon his arrival at the "Bay of Puans" (Green Bay, Wisconsin), Marquette found a village inhabited by three nations, viz: "Miamis, Maskoutens, and Kikabeux." He says:

When I arriv'd there, I was very glad to see a great Cross set up in the middle of the Village, adorn'd with several White Skins, Red Girdles, Bows and Arrows, which that good People had offer'd to the Great *Manitou*, to return him their Thanks for the care he had taken of them during the Winter, and that he had granted them a prosperous Hunting. *Manitou*, is the Name they give in general to all Spirits whom they think to be above the Nature of Man.

Marquette was without doubt ignorant of the fact that the cross is the sacred post, and the symbol of the fourth degree of the Midē′wiwin, as will be fully explained in connection with that grade of the society. The erroneous conclusion that the cross was erected as an evidence of the adoption of Christianity, and possibly as a compliment to the visitor, was a natural one on the part of the priest, but this same symbol of the Midē′ Society had probably been erected and bedecked with barbaric emblems and weapons months before anything was known of him.

The result of personal investigations among the Ojibwa, conducted during the years 1887, 1888 and 1889, are presented in the accompanying paper. The information was obtained from a number of the chief Midē′ priests living at Red Lake and White Earth reservations, as well as from members of the society from other reservations, who visited the last named locality during the three years. Special mention of the peculiarity of the music recorded will be made at the proper place; and it may here be said that in no instance was the use of colors detected, in any birch-bark or other records or mnemonic songs, simply to heighten the artistic effect; though the reader would be led by an examination of the works of Schoolcraft to believe this to be a common practice. Col. Garrick Mallery; U.S. Army, in a paper read before the Anthropological Society of 156 Washington, District of Columbia, in 1888, says, regarding this subject:

The general character of his voluminous publications has not been such as to assure modern critics of his accuracy, and the wonderful minuteness, as well as comprehension, attributed by him to the Ojibwa hieroglyphs has been generally regarded of late with suspicion. It was considered in the Bureau of Ethnology an important duty to ascertain how much of truth existed in these remarkable accounts, and for that purpose its pictographic specialists, myself and Dr. W. J. Hoffman as assistant, were last summer directed to proceed to the most favorable points in the present habitat of the tribe, namely, the northern region of Minnesota and Wisconsin, to ascertain how much was yet to be discovered. *** The general results of the comparison of Schoolcraft's statements with what is now found shows that, in substance, he told the truth, but with much exaggeration and coloring. The word "coloring" is particularly appropriate, because, in his copious illustrations, various colors were used freely with apparent significance, whereas, in fact, the general rule in regard to the birch-bark rolls was that they were never colored at all; indeed, the bark was not adapted to coloration. The metaphorical coloring was also used by him in a manner which, to any thorough student of the Indian philosophy and religion, seems absurd. Metaphysical expressions are attached to some of the devices, or, as he calls them, symbols, which, could never have been entertained by a people in the stage of culture of the Ojibwa.

SHAMANS.

There are extant among the Ojibwa Indians three classes of mystery men, termed respectively and in order of importance the Midē′, the Jĕs′sakkīd′, and the Wâbĕnō′, but before proceeding to elaborate in detail the Society of the Midē′, known as the Midē′wiwin, a brief description of the last two is necessary.

The term Wâbĕnō′ has been explained by various intelligent Indians as signifying "Men of the dawn," "Eastern men," etc. Their profession is not thoroughly understood, and their number is so extremely limited that but little information respecting them can be obtained. Schoolcraft,[5] in referring to the several classes of Shamans, says "there is a third form or rather modification of the medawin, *** the Wâbĕnō′; a term denoting a kind of midnight orgies, which is regarded as a corruption of the Meda." This writer furthermore remarks[6] that "it is stated by judicious persons among themselves to be of modern origin. They regard it as a degraded form of the mysteries of the Meda."

From personal investigation it has been ascertained that a Wâbĕnō′ does not affiliate with others of his class so as to constitute a society, but indulges his pretensions individually. A Wâbĕnō′ is primarily prompted by dreams or visions which may occur during his youth, for which purpose he leaves his village to fast for an indefinite number of days. It is positively affirmed that evil man′idōs favor his desires, 157 and apart from his general routine of furnishing "hunting medicine," "love powders," etc., he pretends also to practice medical magic. When a hunter has been successful through the supposed assistance of the Wâbĕnō′, he supplies the latter with part of the game, when, in giving a feast to his tutelary daimon, the Wâbĕnō′ will invite a number of friends, but all who desire to come are welcome. This feast is given at night; singing and dancing are boisterously indulged in, and the Wâbĕnō′, to sustain his reputation, entertains his visitors with a further exhibition of his skill. By the use of plants he is alleged to be enabled to take up and handle with impunity red-hot stones and burning brands, and without evincing the slightest discomfort it is said that he will bathe his hands in boiling water, or even boiling maple sirup. On account of such performances the general impression prevails among the Indians that the Wâbĕnō′ is a "dealer in fire," or "fire-handler." Such exhibitions always terminate at the approach of day. The number of these pretenders who are not members of the Midē′wiwin, is very limited; for instance, there are at present but two or three at White Earth Reservation and none at Leech Lake.

As a general rule, however, the Wâběnō´ will seek entrance into the Midē´wiwin when he becomes more of a specialist in the practice of medical magic, incantations, and the exorcism of malevolent man´idōs, especially such as cause disease.

The Jěs´sakkīd´ is a seer and prophet; though commonly designated a "juggler," the Indians define him as a "revealer of hidden truths." There is no association whatever between the members of this profession, and each practices his art singly and alone whenever a demand is made and the fee presented. As there is no association, so there is no initiation by means of which one may become a Jěs´sakkīd´. The gift is believed to be given by the thunder god, or Animiki´, and then only at long intervals and to a chosen few. The gift is received during youth, when the fast is undertaken and when visions appear to the individual. His renown depends upon his own audacity and the opinion of the tribe. He is said to possess the power to look into futurity; to become acquainted with the affairs and intentions of men; to prognosticate the success or misfortune of hunters and warriors, as well as other affairs of various individuals, and to call from any living human being the soul, or, more strictly speaking, the shadow, thus depriving the victim of reason, and even of life. His power consists in invoking, and causing evil, while that of the Midē´ is to avert it; he attempts at times to injure the Midē´ but the latter, by the aid of his superior man´idos, becomes aware of, and averts such premeditated injury. It sometimes happens that the demon possessing a patient is discovered, but the Midē´ alone has the power to expel him. The exorcism of demons is one of the chief pretensions of this personage, and evil spirits are sometimes removed 158 by sucking them through tubes, and startling tales are told how the Jěs´sakkīd´ can, in the twinkling of an eye, disengage himself of the most complicated tying of cords and ropes, etc. The lodge used by this class of men consists of four poles planted in the ground, forming a square of three or four feet and upward in diameter, around which are wrapped birch bark, robes, or canvas in such a way as to form an upright cylinder. Communion is held with the turtle, who is the most powerful man´idō of the Jěs´sakkīd´, and through him, with numerous other malevolent man´idōs, especially the Animiki´, or thunder-bird. When the prophet has seated himself within his lodge the structure begins to sway violently from side to side, loud thumping noises are heard within, denoting the arrival of man´idōs, and numerous voices and laughter are distinctly audible to those without. Questions may then be put to the prophet and, if everything be favorable, the response is not long in coming. In his notice of the Jěs´sakkīd´, Schoolcraft affirms[7] that "while he thus exercises the functions of a prophet, he is also a member of the highest class of the fraternity of the Midâwin—a society of men who exercise the medical art on the principles of magic and incantations." The fact is that there is not the slightest connection between the practice of the Jěs´sakkīd´ and that of the Midē´wiwin, and it is seldom, if at all, that a Midē´ becomes a Jěs´sakkīd´, although the latter sometimes gains admission into the Midē´wiwin, chiefly with the intention of strengthening his power with his tribe.

The number of individuals of this class who are not members of the Midē´wiwin is limited, though greater than that of the Wâběnō´. An idea of the proportion of numbers of the respective classes may be formed by taking the case of Menomoni Indians, who are in this respect upon the same plane as the Ojibwa. That tribe numbers about fifteen hundred, the Midē´ Society consisting, in round numbers, of one hundred members, and among the entire population there are but two Wâběnō´ and five Jěs´sakkīd´.

It is evident that neither the Wâběnō´ nor the Jěs´sakkīd´ confine themselves to the mnemonic songs which are employed during their ceremonial performances, or even prepare them to any extent. Such bark records as have been observed or recorded, even after most careful research and examination extending over the field seasons of three years, prove to have been the property of Wâběnō´ and Jěs´sakkīd´, who were also Midē´. It is probable that those who practice either of the first two forms of ceremonies and nothing else are familiar with and may employ for their own information certain mnemonic records; but they are limited to the characteristic formulæ of exorcism, as their practice varies and is subject to changes according to circumstances and the requirements and wants of the applicant when words are chanted to accord therewith.

159 Some examples of songs used by Jěs´sakkīd´, after they have become Midē´, will be given in the description of the several degrees of the Midē´wiwin.

There is still another class of persons termed Mashkī´kīkē´winĭnĭ, or herbalists, who are generally denominated "medicine men," as the Ojibwa word implies. Their calling is a simple one, and consists in knowing the mysterious properties of a variety of plants, herbs, roots, and berries, which are revealed upon application and for a fee. When there is an administration of a remedy for a given complaint, based upon true scientific principles, it is only in consequence of such practice having been acquired from the whites, as it has usually been the custom of the Catholic Fathers to utilize all ordinary and available remedies for the treatment of the common disorders of life. Although these herbalists are aware that certain plants or roots will produce a specified effect upon the human system, they attribute the benefit to the fact that such remedies are distasteful and injurious to the demons who are present in the system and to whom the disease is attributed. Many of these herbalists are found among women, also; and these, too, are generally members of the Midē´wiwin. In Fig. 1 is shown an herbalist preparing a mixture.

herbalist

Fig. 1.—Herbalist preparing medicine and treating patient.

160 The origin of the Midē´wiwin

or Midē′ Society, commonly, though erroneously, termed Grand Medicine Society, is buried in obscurity. In the Jesuit Relations, as early as 1642, frequent reference is made to sorcerers, jugglers, and persons whose faith, influence, and practices are dependent upon the assistance of "Manitous," or mysterious spirits; though, as there is no discrimination made between these different professors of magic, it is difficult positively to determine which of the several classes were met with at that early day. It is probable that the Jĕs′sakkīd′, or juggler, and the Midē′, or Shaman, were referred to.

The Midē′, in the true sense of the word, is a Shaman, though he has by various authors been termed powwow, medicine man, priest, seer, prophet, etc. Among the Ojibwa the office is not hereditary; but among the Menomoni a curious custom exists, by which some one is selected to fill the vacancy one year after the death of a Shaman. Whether a similar practice prevailed among other tribes of the Algonkian linguistic stock can be ascertained only by similar research among the tribes constituting that stock.

Among the Ojibwa, however, a substitute is sometimes taken to fill the place of one who has been prepared to receive the first degree of the Midē′wiwin, or Society of the Midē′, but who is removed by death before the proper initiation has been conferred. This occurs when a young man dies, in which case his father or mother may be accepted as a substitute. This will be explained in more detail under the caption of Dzhibai′ Midē′wigân or "Ghost Lodge," a collateral branch of the Midē′wiwin.

As I shall have occasion to refer to the work of the late Mr. W. W. Warren, a few words respecting him will not be inappropriate. Mr. Warren was an Ojibwa mixed blood, of good education, and later a member of the legislature of Minnesota. His work, entiled "History of the Ojibwa Nation," was published in Vol. V of the Collections of the Minnesota Historical Society, St. Paul, 1885, and edited by Dr. E. D. Neill. Mr. Warren's work is the result of the labor of a lifetime among his own people, and, had he lived, he would undoubtedly have added much to the historical material of which the printed volume chiefly consists. His manuscript was completed about the year 1852, and he died the following year. In speaking of the Society of the Midē′,8 he says:

The grand rite of Me-da-we-win (or, as we have learned to term it, "Grand Medicine,")and the beliefs incorporated therein, are not yet fully understood by the whites. This important custom is still shrouded in mystery even to my own eyes, though I have taken much pains to inquire and made use of every advantage possessed by speaking their language perfectly, being related to them, possessing their friendship and intimate confidence has given me, and yet I frankly acknowledge that I stand as yet, as it were, on the threshold of the Me-da-we lodge. I believe, however, that I have obtained full as much and more general and true information 161 on this matter than any other person who has written on the subject, not excepting a great and standard author, who, to the surprise of many who know the Ojibways well, has boldly asserted in one of his works that he has been regularly initiated into the mysteries of this rite, and is a member of the Me-da-we Society. This is certainly an assertion hard to believe in the Indian country; and when the old initiators or Indian priests are told of it they shake their heads in incredulity that a white man should ever have been allowed *in truth* to become a member of their Me-da-we lodge.

An entrance into the lodge itself, while the ceremonies are being enacted, has sometimes been granted through courtesy; though this does not initiate a person into the mysteries of the creed, nor does it make him a member of the Society.

These remarks pertaining to the pretensions of "a great and standard authority" have reference to Mr. Schoolcraft, who among numerous other assertions makes the following, in the first volume of his Information Respecting the Indian Tribes of the United States, Philadelphia, 1851, p. 361, viz:

I had observed the exhibitions of the Medawin, and the exactness and studious ceremony with which its rites were performed in 1820 in the region of Lake Superior; and determined to avail myself of the advantages of my official position, in 1822, when I returned as a Government agent for the tribes, to make further inquiries into its principles and mode of proceeding. And for this purpose I had its ceremonies repeated in my office, under the secrecy of closed doors, with every means of both correct interpretation and of recording the result. Prior to this transaction I had observed in the hands of an Indian of the Odjibwa tribe one of those symbolic tablets of pictorial notation which have been sometimes called "music boards," from the fact of their devices being sung off by the initiated of the Meda Society. This constituted the object of the explanations, which, in accordance with the positive requisitions of the leader of the society and three other initiates, was thus ceremoniously made.

This statement is followed by another,9 in which Mr. Schoolcraft, in a foot-note, affirms:

Having in 1823 been myself admitted to the class of a Meda by the Chippewas, and taken the initiatory step of a Sagima and Jesukaid in each of the other fraternities, and studied their pictographic system with great care and good helps, I may speak with the more decision on the subject.

Mr. Schoolcraft presents a superficial outline of the initiatory ceremonies as conducted during his time, but as the description is meager, notwithstanding that there is every evidence that the ceremonies were conducted with more completeness and elaborate dramatization nearly three-quarters of a century ago than at the present day, I shall not burden this paper with useless repetition, but present the subject as conducted within the last three years.

Mr. Warren truly says:

In the Me-da-we rite is incorporated most that is ancient amongst them—songs and traditions that have descended not orally, but in hieroglyphs, for at least a long time of generations. In this rite is also perpetuated the purest and most ancient idioms of their language, which differs somewhat from that of the common everyday use.

162 As the ritual of the Midē´wiwin is based to a considerable extent upon traditions pertaining to the cosmogony and genesis and to the thoughtful consideration by the Good Spirit for the Indian, it is looked upon by them as "their religion," as they themselves designate it.

In referring to the rapid changes occurring among many of the Western tribes of Indians, and the gradual discontinuance of aboriginal ceremonies and customs, Mr. Warren remarks10 in reference to the Ojibwa:

Even among these a change is so rapidly taking place, caused by a close contact with the white race, that ten years hence it will be too late to save the traditions of their forefathers from total oblivion. And even now it is with great difficulty that genuine information can be obtained of them. Their aged men are fast falling into their graves, and they carry with them the records of the past history of their people; they are the initiators of the grand rite of religious belief which they believe the Great Spirit has granted to his red children to secure them long life on earth and life hereafter; and in the bosoms of these old men are locked up the original secrets of this their most ancient belief. ***

They fully believe, and it forms part of their religion, that the world has once been covered by a deluge, and that we are now living on what they term the "new earth." This idea is fully accounted for by their vague traditions; and in their Me-da-we-win or religion, hieroglyphs are used to denote this second earth.

Furthermore,

They fully believe that the red man mortally angered the Great Spirit which caused the deluge, and at the commencement of the new earth it was only through the medium and intercession of a powerful being, whom they denominate Manab-o-sho, that they were allowed to exist, and means were given them whereby to subsist and support life; and a code of religion was more lately bestowed on them, whereby they could commune with the offended Great Spirit, and ward off the approach and ravages of death.

It may be appropriate in this connection to present the description given by Rev. Peter Jones of the Midē´ priests and priestesses. Mr. Jones was an educated Ojibwa Episcopal clergyman, and a member of the Missasauga—i.e., the Eagle totemic division of that tribe of Indians living in Canada. In his work11 he states:

Each tribe has its medicine men and women—an order of priesthood consulted and employed in all times of sickness. These powwows are persons who are believed to have performed extraordinary cures, either by the application of roots and herbs or by incantations. When an Indian wishes to be initiated into the order of a powwow, in the first place he pays a large fee to the faculty. He is then taken into the woods, where he is taught the names and virtues of the various useful plants; next he is instructed how to chant the medicine song, and how to pray, which prayer is a vain repetition offered up to the Master of Life, or to some munedoo whom the afflicted imagine they have offended.

The powwows are held in high veneration by their deluded brethren; not so much for their knowledge of medicine as for the magical power which they are supposed to possess. It is for their interest to lead these credulous people to believe that they can at pleasure hold intercourse with the munedoos, who are ever ready to give them whatever information they require.

163 The Ojibwa believe in a multiplicity of spirits, or man´idōs, which inhabit all space and every conspicuous object in nature. These man´idōs, in turn, are subservient to superior ones, either of a charitable and benevolent character or those which are malignant and aggressive. The chief or superior man´idō is termed Ki´tshi Man´idō—Great Spirit—approaching to a great extent the idea of the God of the Christian religion; the second in their estimation is Dzhe Man´idō, a benign being upon whom they look as the guardian spirit of the Midē´wiwin and through whose divine provision the sacred rites of the Midē´wiwin were granted to man. The Ani´miki or Thunder God is, if not the supreme, at least one of the greatest of the malignant man´idōs, and it is from him that the Jĕs´sakkīd´ are believed to obtain their powers of evil doing. There is one other, to whom special reference will be made, who abides in and rules the "place of shadows," the hereafter he is known as Dzhibai´ Man´idō—Shadow Spirit, or more commonly Ghost Spirit. The name of Ki´tshi Man´idō is never mentioned but with reverence, and thus only in connection with the rite of Midē´wiwin, or a sacred feast, and always after making an offering of tobacco.

The first important event in the life of an Ojibwa youth is his first fast. For this purpose he will leave his home for some secluded spot in the forest where he will continue to fast for an indefinite number of days; when reduced by abstinence from food he enters a hysterical or ecstatic state in which he may have visions and hallucinations. The spirits which the Ojibwa most desire to see in these dreams are those of mammals and birds, though any object, whether animate or inanimate, is considered a good omen. The object which first appears is adopted as the personal mystery, guardian spirit, or tutelary daimon of the entranced, and is never mentioned by him without first making a sacrifice. A small effigy of this man´idō is made, or its outline drawn upon a small piece of birch bark, which is carried suspended by a string around the neck, or if the wearer be a Midē´ he carries it in his "medicine bag" or pinji´-gosân. The future course of life of the faster is governed by his dream; and it sometimes occurs that because of giving an imaginary importance to the occurrence, such as beholding, during the trance some powerful man´idō or other object held in great reverence by the members of the Midē´ Society, the faster first becomes impressed with the idea of becoming a Midē´. Thereupon he makes application to a prominent Midē´ priest, and seeks his advice as to the necessary course to be pursued to attain his desire. If the Midē´ priest considers with favor the application, he consults with his confrères and action is taken, and the questions of the requisite preliminary instructions, fees, and presents, etc., are formally discussed. If the Midē´ priests are in accord with the desires of the applicant an instructor or preceptor is designated, to whom he must present himself 164 and make an agreement as to the amount of preparatory information to be acquired and the fees and other presents to be given in return. These fees have nothing whatever to do with the presents which must be presented to the Midē´ priests previous to his initiation as a member of the society, the latter being collected during the time that is devoted to preliminary instruction, which period usually extends over several years. Thus ample time is found for hunting, as skins and peltries, of which those not required as presents may be exchanged for blankets, tobacco, kettles, guns, etc., obtainable from the trader. Sometimes a number of years are spent in preparation for the first degree of the Midē´wiwin, and there are many who have impoverished themselves in the payment of fees and the preparation for the feast to which all visiting priests are also invited.

Should an Indian who is not prompted by a dream wish to join the society he expresses to the four chief officiating priests a desire to purchase a mī´gis, which is the sacred symbol of the society and consists of a small white shell, to which reference will be made further on. His application follows the same course as in the preceding instance, and the same course is pursued also when a Jĕs´sakkīd´ or a Wâbĕnō´ wishes to become a Midē´.

MIDĒ´WIWIN.

The Midē´wiwin—Society of the Midē´ or Shamans—consists of an indefinite number of Midē´ of both sexes. The society is graded into four separate and distinct degrees, although there is a general impression prevailing even among certain members that any degree beyond the first is practically a mere repetition. The greater power attained by one in making advancement depends upon the fact of his having submitted to "being shot at with the medicine sacks" in the hands of the officiating priests. This may be the case at this late day in certain localities, but from personal experience it has been learned that there is considerable variation in the dramatization of the ritual. One circumstance presents itself forcibly to the careful observer, and that is that the greater number of repetitions of the phrases chanted by the Midē´ the greater is felt to be the amount of inspiration and power of the performance. This is true also of some of the lectures in which reiteration and prolongation in time of delivery aids very much in forcibly impressing the candidate and other observers with the importance and sacredness of the ceremony.

It has always been customary for the Midē´ priests to preserve birch-bark records, bearing delicate incised lines to represent pictorially the ground plan of the number of degrees to which the owner is entitled. Such records or charts are sacred and are never exposed to the public view, being brought forward for inspection only when 165 an accepted candidate has paid his fee, and then only after necessary preparation by fasting and offerings of tobacco.

key to plate III
Plate III. Red Lake And Leech Lake Records (*key*).
Complete Plate

During the year 1887, while at Red Lake, Minnesota, I had the good fortune to discover the existence of an old birch-bark chart, which, according to the assurances of the chief and assistant Midē´ priests, had never before been exhibited to a white man, nor even to an Indian unless he had become a regular candidate. This chart measures 7 feet 1½ inches in length and 18 inches in width, and is made of five pieces of birch bark neatly and securely stitched together by means of thin, flat strands of bass wood. At each end are two thin strips of wood, secured transversely by wrapping and stitching with thin strands of bark, so as to prevent splitting and fraying of the ends of the record. Pl. III A , is a reproduction of the design referred to.

It had been in the keeping of Skwĕkŏ´mĭk, to whom it was intrusted at the death of his father-in-law, the latter, in turn, having received it in 1825 from Badâ´san, the Grand Shaman and chief of the Winnibē´goshish Ojibwa.

It is affirmed that Badâ´san had received the original from the Grand Midē´ priest at La Pointe, Wisconsin, where, it is said, the Midē´wiwin was at that time held annually and the ceremonies conducted in strict accordance with ancient and traditional usage.

The present owner of this record has for many years used it in the preliminary instruction of candidates. Its value in this respect is very great, as it presents to the Indian a pictorial résumé of the traditional history of the origin of the Midē´wiwin, the positions occupied by the various guardian man´idos in the several degrees, and the order of procedure in study and progress of the candidate. On account of the isolation of the Red Lake Indians and their long continued, independent ceremonial observances, changes have gradually occurred so that there is considerable variation, both in the pictorial representation and the initiation, as compared with the records and ceremonials preserved at other reservations. The reason of this has already been given.

A detailed description of the above mentioned record, will be presented further on in connection with two interesting variants which were subsequently obtained at White Earth, Minnesota. On account of the widely separated location of many of the different bands of the Ojibwa, and the establishment of independent Midē´ societies, portions of the ritual which have been forgotten by one set may be found to survive at some other locality, though at the expense of some other fragments of tradition or ceremonial. No satisfactory account of the tradition of the origin of the Indians has been obtained, but such information as it was possible to procure will be submitted.

166 In all of their traditions pertaining to the early history of the tribe these people are termed A-nish´-in-â´-bēg—original people—a term surviving also among the Ottawa, Patawatomi, and Menomoni, indicating that the tradition of their westward migration was extant prior to the final separation of these tribes, which is supposed to have occurred at Sault Ste. Marie.

Mi´nabō´zho (Great Rabbit), whose name occurs in connection with most of the sacred rites, was the servant of Dzhe Man´idō, the Good Spirit, and acted in the capacity of intercessor and mediator. It is generally supposed that it was to his good offices that the Indian owes life and the good things necessary to his health and subsistence.

The tradition of Mi´nabō´zho and the origin of the Midē´wiwin, as given in connection with the birch-bark record obtained at Red Lake (Pl. III A), is as follows:

When Mi´nabō´zho, the servant of Dzhe Man´idō, looked down upon the earth he beheld human beings, the Ani´shinâ´bēg, the ancestors of the Ojibwa. They occupied the four quarters of the earth—the northeast, the southeast, the southwest, and the northwest. He saw how helpless they were, and desiring to give them the means of warding off the diseases with which they were constantly afflicted, and to provide them with animals and plants to serve as food and with other comforts, Mi´nabō´zho remained thoughtfully hovering over the center of the earth, endeavoring to devise some means of communicating with them, when he heard something laugh, and perceived a dark object appear upon the surface of the water to the west (No. 2). He could not recognize its form, and while watching it closely it slowly disappeared from view. It next appeared in the north (No. 3), and after a short lapse of time again disappeared. Mi´nabō´zho hoped it would once show itself upon the surface of the water, which it did in the east (No. 4). Then Mi´nabō´zho wished that it might approach him, so as to permit him to communicate with it. When it disappeared from view in the east and made its reappearance in the south (No. 1), Mi´nabō´zho asked it to come to the center of the earth that he might behold it. Again it disappeared from view, and after reappearing in the west Mi´nabō´zho observed it slowly approaching the center of the earth (i.e., the centre of the circle), when he descended and saw it was the Otter, now one of the sacred man´idōs of the Midē´wiwin. Then Mi´nabō´zho instructed the Otter in the mysteries of the Midē´wiwin, and gave him at the same time the sacred rattle to be used at the side of the sick; the sacred Midē´ drum to be used during the ceremonial of initiation and at sacred feasts, and tobacco, to be employed in invocations and in making peace.

The place where Mi´nabō´zho descended was an island in the middle of a large body of water, and the Midē´ who is feared by all the others is called Mini´sino´shkwe (He-who-lives-on-the-island). Then 167 Mi´nabō´zho built a Midē´wigân (sacred Midē´ lodge), and taking his drum he beat upon it and sang a Midē´ song, telling the Otter that Dzhe Man´idō had decided to help the Anishinâ´bōg, that they might always have life and an abundance of food and other things necessary for their comfort. Mi´nabō´zho then took the Otter into the Midē´wigân and conferred upon him the secrets of the Midē´wiwin, and with his Midē´ bag shot the sacred mī´gis into his body that he might have immortality and be able to confer these secrets to his kinsmen, the Anishinâ´bēg.

The mī´gis is considered the sacred symbol of the Midē´wigân, and may consist of any small white shell, though the one believed to be similar to the one mentioned in the above tradition resembles the cowrie, and the ceremonies of initiation as carried out in the Midē´wiwin at this day are believed to be similar to those enacted by Mi´nabō´zho and the Otter. It is admitted by all the Midē´ priests whom I have consulted that much of the information has been lost through the death of their aged predecessors, and they feel convinced that ultimately all of the sacred character of the work will be forgotten or lost through the adoption of new religions by the young people and the death of the Midē´ priests, who, by the way, decline to accept Christian teachings, and are in consequence termed "pagans."

My instructor and interpreter of the Red Lake chart added other information in explanation of the various characters represented thereon, which I present herewith. The large circle at the right side of the chart denotes the earth as beheld by Mi´nabō´zho, while the Otter appeared at the square projections at Nos. 1, 2, 3, and 4; the semicircular appendages between these are the four quarters of the earth, which are inhabited by the Ani´shinâ´bēg, Nos. 5, 6, 7, and 8. Nos. 9 and 10 represent two of the numerous malignant man´idōs, who endeavor to prevent entrance into the sacred structure and mysteries of the Midē´wiwin. The oblong squares, Nos. 11 and 12, represent the outline of the first degree of the society, the inner corresponding lines being the course traversed during initiation. The entrance to the lodge is directed toward the east, the western exit indicating the course toward the next higher degree. The four human forms at Nos. 13, 14, 15, and 16 are the four officiating Midē´ priests whose services are always demanded at an initiation. Each is represented as having a rattle. Nos. 17, 18, and 19 indicate the cedar trees, one of each of this species being planted near the outer angles of a Midē´ lodge. No. 20 represents the ground. The outline of the bear at No. 21 represents the Makwa´ Man´idō, or Bear Spirit, one of the sacred Midē´ man´idōs, to which the candidate must pray and make offerings of tobacco, that he may compel the malevolent spirits to draw away from the entrance to the Midē´wigân, which is shown in No. 28. Nos 23 and 24 represent the sacred drum which 168 the candidate must use when chanting the prayers, and two offerings must be made, as indicated by the number two.

After the candidate has been admitted to one degree, and is prepared to advance to the second, he offers three feasts, and chants three prayers to the

Makwa' Man'idō, or Bear Spirit (No. 22), that the entrance (No. 29) to that degree may be opened to him. The feasts and chants are indicated by the three drums shown at Nos. 25, 26, and 27.

Nos. 30, 31, 32, 33, and 34 are five Serpent Spirits, evil man'idōs who oppose a Midē''s progress, though after the feasting and prayers directed to the Makwa' Man'idō have by him been deemed sufficient the four smaller Serpent Spirits move to either side of the path between the two degrees, while the larger serpent (No. 32) raises its body in the middle so as to form an arch, beneath which passes the candidate on his way to the second degree.

Nos. 35, 36, 46, and 47 are four malignant Bear Spirits, who guard the entrance and exit to the second degree, the doors of which are at Nos. 37 and 49. The form of this lodge (No. 38) is like the preceding; but while the seven Midē' priests at Nos. 39, 40, 41, 42, 43, 44, and 45 simply indicate that the number of Midē' assisting at this second initiation are of a higher and more sacred class of personages than in the first degree, the number designated having reference to quality and intensity rather than to the actual number of assistants, as specifically shown at the top of the first degree structure.

When the Midē' is of the second degree, he receives from Dzhe Man'idō supernatural powers as shown in No. 48. The lines extending upward from the eyes signify that he can look into futurity; from the ears, that he can hear what is transpiring at a great distance; from the hands, that he can touch for good or for evil friends and enemies at a distance, however remote; while the lines extending from the feet denote his ability to traverse all space in the accomplishment of his desires or duties. The small disk upon the breast of the figure denotes that a Midē' of this degree has several times had the mī'gis—life—"shot into his body," the increased size of the spot signifying amount or quantity of influence obtained thereby.

No. 50 represents a Mi'tsha Midē' or Bad Midē', one who employs his powers for evil purposes. He has the power of assuming the form of any animal, in which guise he may destroy the life of his victim, immediately after which he resumes his human form and appears innocent of any crime. His services are sought by people who wish to encompass the destruction of enemies or rivals, at however remote a locality the intended victim may be at the time. An illustration representing the modus operandi of his performance is reproduced and explained in Fig. 24, page 238.

Persons possessed of this power are sometimes termed witches, special reference to whom is made elsewhere. The illustration, No. 169 50, represents such an individual in his disguise of a bear, the characters at Nos. 51 and 52 denoting footprints of a bear made by him, impressions of which are sometimes found in the vicinity of lodges occupied by his intended victims. The trees shown upon either side of No. 50 signify a forest, the location usually sought by bad Midē' and witches.

If a second degree Midē' succeeds in his desire to become a member of the third degree, he proceeds in a manner similar to that before described; he gives feasts to the instructing and four officiating Midē', and offers prayers to Dzhe Man'idō for favor and success. No. 53 denotes that the candidate now personates the bear—not one of the malignant man'idōs, but one of the sacred man'idōs who are believed to be present during the ceremonials of initiation of the second degree. He is seated before his sacred drum, and when the proper time arrives the Serpent Man'idō (No. 54)—who has until this opposed his advancement—now arches its body, and beneath it he crawls and advances toward the door (No. 55) of the third degree (No. 56) of the Midē'wiwin, where he encounters two (Nos. 57 and 58) of the four Panther Spirits, the guardians of this degree.

Nos. 61 to 76 indicate midē' spirits who inhabit the structure of this degree, and the number of human forms in excess of those shown in connection with the second degree indicates a correspondingly higher and more sacred character. When an Indian has passed this, initiation he becomes very skillful in his profession of a Midē'. The powers which he possessed in the second degree may become augmented. He is represented in No. 77 with arms extended, and with lines crossing his body and arms denoting darkness and obscurity, which signifies his ability to grasp from the invisible world the knowledge and means to accomplish extraordinary deeds. He feels more confident of prompt response and assistance from the sacred man'idōs and his knowledge of them becomes more widely extended.

Nos. 59 and 60 are two of the four Panther Spirits who are the special guardians of the third degree lodge.

To enter the fourth and highest degree of the society requires a greater number of feasts than before, and the candidate, who continues to personate the Bear Spirit, again uses his sacred drum, as he is shown sitting before it in No. 78, and chants more prayers to Dzhe Man'idō for his favor. This degree is guarded by the greatest number and the most powerful of malevolent spirits, who make a last effort to prevent a candidate's entrance at the door (No. 79) of the fourth degree structure (No. 80). The chief opponents to be overcome, through the assistance of Dzhe Man'idō, are two Panther Spirits (Nos. 81 and 82) at the eastern entrance, and two Bear Spirits (Nos. 83 and 84) at the western exit. Other bad spirits are about the structure, who frequently gain possession and are then enabled to make strong and prolonged resistance to the candidate's entrance. 170 The chiefs of this group of malevolent beings are Bears (Nos. 88 and 96), the Panther (No. 91), the Lynx (No. 97), and many others whose names they have forgotten, their positions being indicated at Nos. 85, 86, 87, 89, 90, 92, 93, 94, and 95, all but the last resembling characters ordinarily employed to designate serpents.

The power with which it is possible to become endowed after passing through the fourth degree is expressed by the outline of a human figure (No. 98), upon which are a number of spots indicating that the body is covered with the mī′gis or sacred shells, symbolical of the Midē′wiwin. These spots designate the places where the Midē′ priests, during the initiation, shot into his body the mī′gis and the lines connecting them in order that all the functions of the several corresponding parts or organs of the body may be exercised.

The ideal fourth degree Midē′ is presumed to be in a position to accomplish the greatest feats in necromancy and magic. He is not only endowed with the power of reading the thoughts and intentions of others, as is pictorially indicated by the mī′gis spot upon the top of the head, but to call forth the shadow (soul) and retain it within his grasp at pleasure. At this stage of his pretensions, he is encroaching upon the prerogatives of the Jĕs′sakkĭd′, and is then recognized as one, as he usually performs within the Jĕs′sakkân or Jĕs′sakkĭd′ lodge, commonly designated "the Jugglery."

The ten small circular objects upon the upper part of the record may have been some personal marks of the original owner; their import was not known to my informants and they do not refer to any portion of the history or ceremonies or the Midē′wiwin.

Extending toward the left from the end of the fourth degree inclosure is an angular pathway (No. 99), which represents the course to be followed by the Midē′ after he has attained this high distinction. On account of his position his path is often beset with dangers, as indicated by the right angles, and temptations which may lead him astray; the points at which he may possibly deviate from the true course of propriety are designated by projections branching off obliquely toward the right and left (No. 100). The ovoid figure (No. 101) at the end of this path is termed Wai-ĕk′-ma-yŏk′—End of the road—and is alluded to in the ritual, as will be observed hereafter, as the end of the world, i.e., the end of the individual's existence. The number of vertical strokes (No. 102) within the ovoid figure signify the original owner to have been a fourth degree Midē′ for a period of 14 years.

The outline of the Midē′wigân (No. 103) not only denotes that the same individual was a member of the Midē′wiwin, but the thirteen vertical strokes shown in Nos. 104 and 105 indicate that he was chief Midē′ priest of the society for that number of years.

The outline of a Midē′wigân as shown at No. 106, with the place upon the interior designating the location of the sacred post (No. 171 107) and the stone (No. 108) against which the sick are placed during the time of treatment, signifies the owner to have practiced his calling of the exorcism of demons. But that he also visited the sick beyond the acknowledged jurisdiction of the society in which he resided, is indicated by the path (No. 109) leading around the sacred inclosure

Upon that portion of the chart immediately above the fourth degree lodge is shown the outline of a Midē′wiwin (No. 110), with a path (No. 114), leading toward the west to a circle (No. 111), within which is another similar structure (No. 112) whose longest diameter is at right angles to the path, signifying that it is built so that its entrance is at the north. This is the Dzhibai′ Midē′wigân or Ghost Lodge

Around the interior of the circle are small V-shaped characters denoting the places occupied by the spirits of the departed, who are presided over by the Dzhibai′ Midē′, literally Shadow Midē′.

No. 113 represents the Kŏ′-kó-kŏ-ō′ (Owl) passing from the Midē′wigân to the Land of the Setting Sun, the place of the dead, upon the road of the dead, indicated by the pathway at No. 114. This man′idō is personated by a candidate for the first degree of the Midē′wiwin when giving a feast to the dead in honor of the shadow of him who had been dedicated to the Midē′wiwin and whose place is now to be taken by the giver of the feast.

Upon the back of the Midē′ record, above described, is the personal record of the original owner, as shown in Pl. III B . Nos. 1, 2, 3, and 4 represent the four degrees of the society into which he has been initiated, or, to use the phraseology of an Ojibwa, "through which he has gone." This "passing through" is further illustrated by the bear tracks, he having personated the Makwa′ Man′idō or Bear Spirit, considered to be the highest and most powerful of the guardian spirits of the fourth degree wigwam.

The illustration presented in Pl. III C represents the outlines of a birch-bark record (reduced to one-third) found among the effects of a lately deceased Midē′ from Leech Lake, Minnesota. This record, together with a number of other curious articles, composed the outfit of the Midē′, but the Rev. James A. Gilfillan of White Earth, through whose courtesy I was permitted to examine the objects, could give me no information concerning their use. Since that time, however, I have had an opportunity of consulting with one of the chief priests of the Leech Lake Society, through whom I have obtained some interesting data concerning them.

The chart represents the owner to have been a Midē′ of the second degree, as indicated by the two outlines of the respective structures at Nos. 1 and 2, the place of the sacred posts being marked at Nos. 3 and 4. Nos. 5, 6, 7, and 8 are Midē′ priests holding their Midē′ bags as in the ceremony of initiation. The disks represented at Nos. 172 9, 10, 11, 12, and 13 denote the sacred drum, which may be used by him during his initiation, while Nos. 14, 15, 16, and 17 denote that he was one of the four officiating priests of the Midē′wigân at his place of residence. Each of these figures is represented as holding their sacred bags as during the ceremonies. No. 18 denotes the path he has been pursuing since he became a Midē′, while at Nos. 19 and 20 diverging lines signify that his course is beset with temptations and enemies, as referred to in the description of the Red Lake chart, Pl. III A .

The remaining objects found among the effects of the Midē′ referred to will be described and figured hereafter.

plate described in text

Plate IV. Sikas′sige's Record.
Larger Plate

The diagram represented on Pl. IV is a reduced copy of a record made by Sikas′sigĕ, a Mille Lacs Ojibwa Midē′ of the second degree, now resident at White Earth.

The chart illustrating pictorially the general plan of the several degrees is a copy of a record in the possession of the chief Midē′ at Mille Lacs in 1830, at which time Sikas′sigĕ, at the age of 10 years, received his first degree. For a number of years thereafter Sikas′sigĕ received continued instruction from his father Baiē′dzhĕk, and although he never publicly received advancement beyond the second degree of the society, his wife became a fourth degree priestess, at whose initiation he was permitted to be present.

plate described in text
Plate V. Origin of Âni′shinâ′bēg.
Larger Plate

Since his residence at White Earth Sikas′sigĕ has become one of the officiating priests of the society at that place. One version given by him of the origin of the Indians is presented in the following tradition, a pictorial representation having also been prepared of which Pl. V is a reduced copy:

In the beginning, Dzhe Man′idō (No. 1), made the Midē′ Man′idōs. He first created two men (Nos. 2 and 3), and two women (Nos. 4 and 5); but they had no power of thought or reason. Then Dzhe Man′idō (No. 1) made them rational beings. He took them in his hands so that they should multiply; he paired them, and from this sprung the Indians. When there were people he placed them upon the earth, but he soon observed that they were subject to sickness, misery, and death, and that unless he provided them with the Sacred Medicine they would soon become extinct.

Between the position occupied by Dzhe Man′idō and the earth were four lesser spirits (Nos. 6, 7, 8, and 9) with whom Dzhe Man′idō decided to commune, and to impart to them the mysteries by which the Indians could be benefited. So he first spoke to a spirit at No. 6, and told him all he had to say, who in turn communicated the same information to No. 7, and he in turn to No. 8, who also communed with No. 9. They all met in council, and determined to call in the four wind gods at Nos. 10, 11, 12, and 13. After consulting as to what would be best for the comfort and welfare of the Indians, these spirits agreed to ask Dzhe Man′idō to communicate the Mystery of the Sacred Medicine to the people.

Dzhe Man′idō then went to the Sun Spirit (No. 14) and asked him to go to the earth and instruct the people as had been decided upon by the council. The Sun Spirit, in the form of a little boy, went to the earth and lived with a woman (No. 15) who had a little boy of her own.

This family went away in the autum to hunt, and during the winter this woman's 173 son died. The parents were so much distressed that they decided to return to the village and bury the body there; so they made preparations to return, and as they traveled along, they would each evening erect several poles upon which the body was placed to prevent the wild beasts from devouring it. When the dead boy was thus hanging upon the poles, the adopted child—who was the Sun Spirit—would play about the camp and amuse himself, and finally told his adopted father he pitied him, and his mother, for their sorrow. The adopted son said he could bring his dead brother to life, whereupon the parents expressed great surprise and desired to know how that could be accomplished.

The adopted boy then had the party hasten to the village, when he said, "Get the women to make a wig′iwam of bark (No. 16), put the dead boy in a covering of birch bark and place the body on the ground in the middle of the wig′iwam." On the next morning after this had been done, the family and friends went into this lodge and seated themselves around the corpse.

When they had all been sitting quietly for some time, they saw through the doorway the approach of a bear (No. 17) which gradually came towards the wig′iwam, entered it, and placed itself before the dead body and said hŭ, hŭ, hŭ, hŭ, when he passed around it towards the left side, with a trembling motion, and as he did so, the body began quivering, and the quivering increased as the bear continued until he had passed around four times, when the body came to life again and stood up. Then the bear called to the father, who was sitting in the distant right-hand corner of the wig′iwam, and addressed to him the following words:

Nōs	ka-nĭ′-wī′-na	wis-shi-na′-bi	a′-sī ya-wī′-an	man′-i-dō
My father	is not	an Indian	not you are	a spirit
Be-mai′-a-mī′-nik	nĭ′-dzhĭ	man′-i-dō	mī-tshí-a-gĭ-zhĭ′-a′-gwa	we-ân′.
Insomuch	my fellow	spirit	now	as you are.
Nōs	a-zhĭ′-gwa	a-sē′-ma	tshí′-a-tō′-yĕk.	A′-mĭ-kŭn′-dem
My father	now	tobacco	you shall put.	He speaks of
mi-ē′-ta	â′-wi-dink′	dzhi-gŏsh′-kwi-tōt′	wen′-dzhi-bi-mâ′-di-zid′-o-ma′	
only once	to be able to do it		why he shall live here	
a-gâ′-wa	bi-mâ-dĭ-zīd′-mi-o-ma′;		nĭ-dzhĭ	man′-i-dō
now	that he scarcely lives;		my fellow	spirit

mí-a-zhĭ′-gwa tshí-gĭ-wĕ′-ân.
now I shall go home.

The little bear boy (No. 17) was the one who did this. He then remained among the Indians (No. 18) and taught them the mysteries of the Grand Medicine (No. 19); and, after he had finished, he told his adopted father that as his mission had been fulfilled he was to return to his kindred spirits, for the Indians would have no need to fear sickness as they now possessed the Grand Medicine which would enable them to live. He also said that his spirit could bring a body to life but once, and he would now return to the sun from which they would feel his influence.

This is called Kwi-wĭ-sĕns´ wĕ-dī´-shĭ-tshī gē-wĭ-nĭp—"Little-boy-his-work."

From subsequent information it was learned that the line No. 22 denotes the earth, and that, being considered as one step in the course of initiation into the Midē´wiwin, three others must be taken before a candidate can be admitted. These steps, or rests, as they are denominated (Nos. 23, 24, and 25), are typified by four distinct gifts of goods, which must be remitted to the Midē´ priests before the ceremony can take place.

Nos. 18 and 19 are repetitions of the figures alluded to in the tradition (Nos. 16 and 17) to signify that the candidate must personate the Makwa´ Man´idō—Bear Spirit—when entering the Midē´wiwin (No. 19). No. 20 is the Midē´ Man´idō as Ki´tshi Man´idō is termed 174 by the Midē´ priests. The presence of horns attached to the head is a common symbol of superior power found in connection with the figures of human and divine forms in many Midē´ songs and other mnemonic records. No. 21 represents the earth's surface, similar to that designated at No. 22.

Upon comparing the preceding tradition of the creation of the Indians with the following, which pertains to the descent to earth of Mi´nabō´zho, there appears to be some discrepancy, which could not be explained by Sikas´sigĕ, because he had forgotten the exact sequence of events; but from information derived from other Midē´ it is evident that there have been joined together two myths, the intervening circumstances being part of the tradition given below in connection with the narrative relating to the chart on Pl. III A.

This chart, which was in possession of the Mille Lacs chief Baiĕ´dzhĕk, was copied by him from that belonging to his preceptor at La Pointe about the year 1800, and although the traditions given by Sikas´sigĕ is similar to the one surviving at Red Lake, the diagram is an interesting variant for the reason that there is a greater amount of detail in the delineation of objects mentioned in the tradition.

By referring to Pl. IV it will be noted that the circle, No. 1, resembles the corresponding circle at the beginning of the record on Pl. III, A, with this difference, that the four quarters of the globe inhabited by the Ani´shinâ´bēg are not designated between the cardinal points at which the Otter appeared, and also that the central island, only alluded to there (Pl. III A), is here inserted.

top of figure 2

bottom of figure 2

The correct manner of arranging the two pictorial records, Pls. III A and IV, is by placing the outline of the earth's surface (Pl. V, No. 21) upon the island indicated in Pl. IV, No. 6, so that the former stands vertically and at right angles to the latter; for the reason that the first half of the tradition pertains to the consultation held between Ki´tshi Man´idō and the four lesser spirits which is believed to have occurred above the earth's surface. According to Sikas´sigĕ the two charts should be joined as suggested in the accompanying illustration, Fig. 2.

Fig. 2. —Sikas´sigĕ's combined charts, showing descent of Min´abō´zho.

complete figure

175 Sikas´sigĕ's explanation of the Mille Lacs chart (Pl. IV) is substantially as follows:

When Mi´nabō´zho descended to the earth to give to the Ani´shinâ´bēg the Midē´wiwin, he left with them this chart, Midē´wigwas´. Ki´tshi Man´idō saw that his people on earth were without the means of protecting themselves against disease and death, so he sent Mi´nabō´zho to give to them the sacred gift. Mi´nabō´zho appeared over the waters and while reflecting in what manner he should be able to communicate with the people, he heard something laugh, just as an otter sometimes cries out. He saw something black appear upon the waters in the west (No. 2) which immediately disappeared beneath the surface again. Then it came up at the northern horizon (No. 3), which pleased Mi´nabō´zho, as he thought he now had some one through whom he might convey the information with which he had been charged by Ki´tshi Man´idō. When the black object disappeared beneath the waters at the north to reappear in the east (No. 4), Mi´nabō´zho desired it would come to him in the middle of the waters, but it disappeared to make its reappearance in the south (No. 5), where it again sank out of sight to reappear in the west (No. 2), when Mi´nabō´zho asked it to approach the center where there was an island (No. 6), which it did. This did Ni´gĭk, the Otter, and for this reason he is given charge of the first degree of the Midē´wiwin (Nos. 35 and 36) where his spirit always abides during initiation and when healing the sick.

Then Ni´gĭk asked Mi´nabō´zho, "Why do you come to this place?" When the latter said, "I have pity on the Ani´shinâ´bēg and wish to give them life; Ki´tshi Man´idō gave me the power to confer upon them the means of protecting themselves against sickness and death, and through you I will give them the Midē´wiwin, and teach them the sacred rites."

Then Mi´nabō´zho built a Midē´wigân in which he instructed the Otter in all the mysteries of the Midē´wiwin. The Otter sat before the door of the Midē´wigân four days (Nos. 7, 8, 9, and 10), sunning himself, after which time he approached the entrance (No. 14), where his progress was arrested (No. 11) by seeing two bad spirits (Nos. 12 and 13) guarding it. Through the powers possessed by Mi´nabō´zho he was enabled to pass these; when he entered the sacred lodge (No. 15), the first object he beheld being the sacred stone (No. 16) against which those who were sick were to be seated, or laid, when undergoing the ceremonial of restoring them to health. He next saw a post (No. 17) painted red with a green band around the top. A sick man would also have to pray 176 to the stone and to the post.

when he is within the Midē′wigân, because within them would be the Midē′ spirits whose help he invoked. The Otter was then taken to the middle of the Midē′wigân where he picked up the mī′gis (No. 18) from among a heap of sacred objects which form part of the gifts given by Ki′tshi Man′idō. The eight man′idōs around the midē′wigân (Nos. 19, 20, 21, 22, 23, 24, 25, and 26) were also sent by Ki′tshi Man′idō to guard the lodge against the entrance of bad spirits.

A life is represented by the line No. 27, the signification of the short lines (Nos. 28, 29, 30, and 31) denoting that the course of human progress is beset by temptations and trials which may be the cause of one's departure from such course of conduct as is deemed proper, and the beliefs taught by the Midē′. When one arrives at middle age (No. 32) his course for the remaining period of life is usually without any special events, as indicated by the plain line No. 27, extending from middle age (No. 32) to the end of one's existence (No. 33). The short lines at Nos. 28, 29, 30, and 31, indicating departure from the path of propriety, terminate in rounded spots and signify, literally, "lecture places," because when a Midē′ feels himself failing in duty or vacillating in faith he must renew professions by giving a feast and lecturing to his confreres, thus regaining his strength to resist evil doing—such as making use of his powers in harming his kinsmen, teaching that which was not given him by Ki′tshi Man′idō through Mi′nabō′zho, etc. His heart must be cleansed and his tongue guarded.

To resume the tradition of the course pursued by the Otter, Sikas′sigĕ said: The Otter then went round the interior of the Midē′wigân (No. 34), and finally seated himself in the west, where Mi′nabō′zho shot into his body the sacred mī′gis, which was in his Midē′ bag. Then Mi′nabō′zho said, "This is your lodge and you shall own it always (Nos. 35 and 36), and eight Midē′ Man′idōs (Nos. 19-26) shall guard it during the night."

The Otter was taken to the entrance (No. 37) of the second degree structure (No. 38), which he saw was guarded by two evil man′idōs (Nos. 39 and 40), who opposed his progress, but who were driven away by Mi′nabō′zho. When the Otter entered at the door he beheld the sacred stone (No. 41) and two posts (Nos. 42, 43), the one nearest to him being painted red with a green band around the top, and another at the middle, with a bunch of little feathers upon the top. The other post (No. 43) was painted red, with only a band of green at the top, similar to the first degree post. Nos. 44 and 45 are the places where sacred objects and gifts are placed. This degree of the Midē′wiwin is guarded at night by twelve Midē′ Man′idōs (Nos. 46 to 57) placed there by Ki′tshi Man′idō, and the degree is owned by the Thunder Bird as shown in Nos. 58, 59.

The circles (Nos. 60, 61, and 62) at either end of the outline of the structure denoting the degree and beneath it are connected by a line (No. 63) as in the preceding degree, and are a mere repetition to denote the course of conduct to be pursued by the Midē′. The points (Nos. 64, 65, 66, and 67), at the termini of the shorter lines, also refer to the feasts and lectures to be given in case of need.

177 To continue the informant's tradition:

When the Otter had passed around the interior of the Midē′wigân four times, he seated himself in the west and faced the degree post, when Mi′nabō′zho again shot into his body the mī′gis, which gave him renewed life. Then the Otter was told to take a "sweat bath" once each day for four successive days, so as to prepare for the next degree. (This number is indicated at the rounded spots at Nos. 68, 69, 70, and 71.)

The third degree of the Midē′wiwin (No. 72) is guarded during the day by two Midē′ spirits (Nos. 73, 74) near the eastern entrance, and by the Makwa′ Man′idō within the inclosure (Nos. 75 and 76), and at night by eighteen Midē′ Man′idōs (Nos. 77 to 94), placed there by Ki′tshi Man′idō. When the Otter approached the entrance (No. 95) he was again arrested in his progress by two evil man′idōs (Nos. 96 and 97), who opposed his admission, but Mi′nibō′zho overcame them and the Otter entered. Just inside of the door, and on each side, the Otter saw a post (Nos. 98 and 99), and at the western door or exit two corresponding posts (Nos. 100 and 101). These symbolized the four legs of the Makwa′ Man′idō, or Bear Spirit, who is the guardian by day and the owner of the third degree. The Otter then observed the sacred stone (No. 102) and the two heaps of sacred objects (Nos. 103 and 104) which Mi′nabō′zho had deposited, and three degree posts (Nos. 105, 106, and 107), the first of which (No. 105) was a plain cedar post with the bark upon it, but sharpened at the top; the second (No. 106), a red post with a green band round the top and one about the middle, as in the second degree; and the third a cross (No. 107) painted red, each of the tips painted green. [The vertical line No. 108 was said to have no relation to anything connected with the tradition.] After the Otter had observed the interior of the Midē′wigân he again made four circuits, after which he took his station in the west, where he seated himself, facing the sacred degree posts. Then Mi′nabō′zho, for the third time, shot into his body the mī′gis, thus adding to the powers which he already possessed, after which he was to prepare for the fourth degree of the Midē′wiwin.

Other objects appearing upon the chart were subsequently explained as follows:

The four trees (Nos. 109, 110, 111, and 112), one of which is planted at each of the four corners of the Midē′wigân, are usually cedar, though pine may be taken as a substitute when the former can not be had. The repetition of the circles Nos. 113, 114, and 115 and connecting line No. 116, with the short lines at Nos. 117, 118, 119, and 120, have the same signification as in the preceding two degrees.

After the Otter had received the third degree he prepared himself for the fourth, and highest, by taking a steam bath once a day for four successive days

(Nos. 121, 122, 123, and 124). Then, as he proceeded toward the Midē′wigân he came to a wig′iwam made of brush (No. 179), which was the nest of Makwa′ Man′idō, the Bear Spirit, who guarded the four doors of the sacred structure.

The four rows of spots have reference to the four entrances of the Midē′wigân of the fourth degree. The signification of the spots near the larger circle, just beneath the "Bear's nest" could not be explained by Sikas′sigĕ, but the row of spots (No. 117) along the horizontal line leading to the entrance of the inclosure were denominated steps, or stages of progress, equal to as many days—one spot denoting one day—which must elapse before the Otter was permitted to view the entrance.

peep-hole post
Fig. 4.—Peep-hole post.

When the Otter approached the fourth degree (No. 118) he came to a short post 178 (No. 119) in which there was a small aperture. The post was painted green on the side from which he approached and red upon the side toward the Midē′wigân [see Fig. 4.] But before he was permitted to look through it he rested and invoked the favor of Ki′tshi Man′idō, that the evil man′idōs might be expelled from his path. Then, when the Otter looked through the post, he saw that the interior of the inclosure was filled with Midē′ Man′idos, ready to receive him and to attend during his initiation. The two Midē′ Man′idos at the outside of the eastern entrance (Nos. 120 and 121) compelled the evil man′idōs (Nos. 122 and 123) to depart and permit the Otter to enter at the door (No. 124). Then the Otter beheld the sacred stone (No. 125) and the five heaps of sacred objects which Minabō′zho had deposited (Nos. 126, 127, 128, 129, and 130) near the four degree posts (Nos. 131, 132, 133, and 134). According to their importance, the first was painted red, with a green band about the top; the second was painted red, with two green bands, one at the top and another at the middle; the third consisted of a cross painted red, with the tips of the arms and the top of the post painted green; while the fourth was a square post, the side toward the east being painted white, that toward the south green, that toward the west red, and that toward the north black.

The two sets of sticks (Nos. 135 and 136) near the eastern and western doors represent the legs of Makwa′ Man′idō, the Bear Spirit. When the Otter had observed all these things he passed round the interior of the Midē′wigân four times, after which he seated himself in the west, facing the degree posts, when Mi′nabō′zho approached him and for the fourth time shot into his body the sacred mī′gis, which gave him life that will endure always. Then Mi′nabō′zho said to the Otter, "This degree belongs to Ki′tshi Man′idō, the Great Spirit (Nos. 137 and 138), who will always be present when you give the sacred rite to any of your people." At night the Midē′ Man′idōs (Nos. 139 to 162) will guard the Midē′wigân, as they are sent by Ki′tshi Man′ido to do so. The Bear's nest (Nos. 163 and 164) just beyond the northern and southern doors (Nos. 165 and 166) of the Midē′wigân are the places where Makwa′ Man′idō takes his station when guarding the doors.

Then the Otter made a wig′iwam and offered four prayers (Nos. 167, 168, 169, and 170) for the rites of the Midē′wiwin, which Ki′tshi Man′idō had given him.

The following supplemental explanations were added by Sikas′sigĕ, viz: The four vertical lines at the outer angles of the lodge structure (Nos. 171, 172, 173, and 174), and four similar ones on the inner corners (Nos. 175, 176, 177, and 178), represent eight cedar trees planted there by the Midē′ at the time of preparing the Midē′wigân for the reception of candidates. The circles Nos. 179, 180, and 181, and the connecting line, are a reproduction of similar ones shown in the three preceding degrees, and signify the course of a Midē′'s life—that it should be without fault and in strict accordance with the teachings of the Midē′wiwin. The short lines, terminating in circles Nos. 182, 183, 184, and 185, allude to temptations which beset the Midē′'s path, and he shall, when so tempted, offer at these points feasts and lectures, or, in other words, "professions of faith." The three lines Nos. 186, 187, and 188, consisting of four 179 spots each, which radiate from the larger circle at No. 179 and that before mentioned at No. 116, symbolize the four bear nests and their respective approaches, which are supposed to be placed opposite the four doors of the fourth degree; and it is obligatory, therefore, for a candidate to enter these four doors on hands and knees when appearing for his initiation and before he finally waits to receive the concluding portion of the ceremony.

migration route
Fig. 5.—
Migration of Ânishinâ′beg.

The illustration presented in Fig. 5 is a reduced copy of a drawing made by Sikas′sigĕ to represent the migration of the Otter toward the west after he had received the rite of the Midē′wiwin. No. 1 refers to the circle upon the large chart on Pl. III in A, No. 1, and signifies the earth's surface as before described. No. 2 in Fig. 5 is a line separating the history of the Midē′wiwin from that of the migration as follows: When the Otter had offered four prayers, as above mentioned, which fact is referred to by the spot No. 3, he disappeared beneath the surface of the water and went toward the west, whither the Ani′shinâ′bĕg followed him, and located at Ottawa Island (No. 4). Here they erected the Midē′wigân and lived for many years. Then the Otter again disappeared beneath the water, and in a short time reappeared at A′wiat′ang (No. 5), when the Midē′wigân was again erected and the sacred rites conducted in accordance with the teachings of Mi′nabō′zho. Thus was an interrupted migration continued, the several resting places being given below in their proper order, at each of which the rites of the Midē′wiwin were conducted in all their purity. The next place to locate at was Mi′shenama′kinagung—Mackinaw (No. 6); then Ne′mikung (No. 7); Kiwe′winang′ (No. 8); Bâwating—

Sault Ste. Marie (No. 9); Tshiwi′towi′ (No. 10); Nega′wadzhĕ′ŭ—Sand Mountain (No. 11), northern shore of Lake Superior; Mi′nisa′wĭk [Mi′nisa′bikkăng]—Island of rocks (No. 12); Kawa′sitshĭuwongk—Foaming rapids (No. 13); Mush′kisi′wi [Mash′kisi′bi]—Bad River (No. 14); Shagawâmikongk—Long-sand-bar-beneath-the-surface (No. 15); Wikwe′dâwonggâ—Sandy Bay (No. 16); Neâ′shiwikongk—Cliff Point (No. 17); Netâ′waya′sink—Little point-of-sandbar (No. 18); A′nibis—Little elm tree (No. 19); Wikup′bimish-literally, Little-island-basswood (No. 20); Makubi′mish—Bear Island (No. 21); Sha′geski′ke′dawan′ga (No. 22); Ni′wigwas′sikongk—The place where bark is peeled (No. 23); Ta′pakwe′ĭkak [Sa′apakwe′shkwaokongk]—The-place-where-lodge-bark-is-obtained (No. 24); Ne′uwesak′kudeze′bi [Ne′wisaku′desi′bi]—Point-deadwood-timber river (No. 25); Anibi′kanzi′bi [modern name, Âsh′kiba′gisi′bi], given respectively as Fish spawn River and Green leaf River (No. 26).

This last-named locality is said to be Sandy Lake, Minnesota, where the Otter appeared for the last time, and where the Midē′wigân was finally located. From La Pointe, as well as from Sandy Lake, the Ojibwa claim to have dispersed in bands over various portions of the territory, as well as into Wisconsin, which final separation into distinct bodies has been the chief cause of the gradual changes found to exist in the ceremonies of the Midē′wiwin.

facial decorations shown in color
Plate VI. Ojibwa Facial Decoration.
According to Sikas′sigĕ, the above account of the initiation of the Otter, by Mi′nabo′zho, was adopted as the course of initiation by the Midē′ priests of the Mille Lacs Society, when he himself received the first degree, 1830. At that time a specific method of facial decoration was pursued by the priests of the respective degrees (Pl. VI), each adopting that pertaining to the highest degree to which he was entitled, viz:

First degree.—A broad band of green across the forehead and a narrow stripe of vermilion across the face, just below the eyes.

Second degree.—A narrow stripe of vermilion across the temples, the eyelids, and the root of the nose, a short distance above which is a similar stripe of green, then another of vermilion, and above this again one of green.

Third degree.—Red and white spots are daubed all over the face, the spots being as large as can be made by the finger tips in applying the colors.

Fourth degree.—Two forms of decoration were admissible; for the first, the face was painted with vermilion, with a stripe of green extending diagonally across it from the upper part of the left temporal region to the lower part of the right cheek; for the second, the face was painted red with two short, horizontal parallel bars of 181 green across the forehead. Either of these was also employed as a sign of mourning by one whose son has been intended for the priesthood of the Midē′wiwin, but special reference to this will be given in connection with the ceremony of the Dzhibai′ Midē′wigân, or Ghost Society.

plate described in text
Plate VIII. Ojibwa's Record.
Larger Plate
On Pl. VIII is presented a reduced copy of the Midē′ chart made by Ojibwa, a Midē′ priest of the fourth degree and formerly a member of the society of the Sandy Lake band of the Mississippi Ojibwa. The illustration is copied from his own chart which he received in 1833 in imitation of that owned by his father, Me′toshi′kōsh; and this last had been received from Lake Superior, presumably La Pointe, many years before.

The illustration of the four degrees are here represented in profile, and shows higher artistic skill than the preceding copies from Red Lake, and Mille Lacs.

The information given by Ojibwa, regarding the characters is as follows:
When Ki′tshi Man′idō had decided to give to the Ani′shinâ′bēg the rites of the Midē′wiwin, he took his Midē′ drum and sang, calling upon the other Man′idōs to join him and to hear what he was going to do. No. 1 represents the abode in the sky of Ki′tshi Man′idō, No. 2, indicating the god as he sits drumming, No. 3. the small spots surrounding the drum denoting the mī′gis with which everything about him is covered. The Midē′ Man′idōs came to him in his Midē′wigân (No. 4), eleven of which appear upon the inside of that structure, while the ten—all but himself—upon the outside (Nos. 5 to 14) are represented as descending to the earth, charged with the means of conferring upon the Ani′shinâbē′g the sacred rite. In the Midē′wigân (No. 4) is shown also the sacred post (No. 15) upon which is perched Kŏ-ko′kŏ-ō—the Owl (No. 16). The line traversing the structure, from side to side, represents the trail leading through it, while the two rings (Nos. 17 and 18) upon the right side of the post indicate respectively the spot where the presents are deposited and the sacred stone—this according to modern practices.

When an Indian is prepared to receive the rights of initiation he prepares a wig′iwam (No. 19) in which he takes a steam bath once each day for four successive days. The four baths and four days are indicated by the number of spots at the floor of the lodge, representing stones. The instructors, employed by him, and the officiating priests of the society are present, one of which (No. 20) may be observed upon the left of the wig′iwam in the act of making an offering of smoke, while the one to the right (No. 21) is drumming and singing. The four officiating priests are visible to either side of the candidate within the structure. The wig′iwams (Nos. 22, 23, 24, and 25) designate the village habitations.

In the evening of the day preceding the initiation, the candidate (No. 26) visits his instructor (No. 27) to receive from him final directions as to the part to be enacted upon the following day. The candidate is shown in the act of carrying with him his pipe, the offering of tobacco being the most acceptable of all gifts. His relatives follow and carry the goods and other presents, some of which are suspended from the branches of the Midē′ tree (No. 28) near the entrance of the first degree structure. The instructor's wig′iwam is shown at No. 29, the two dark circular spots upon the floor showing two of the seats, occupied by instructor and pupil. The figure No. 27 has his left arm elevated, denoting that his conversation pertains to Ki′tshi Man′idō, while in his right hand he holds his Midē′ drum. Upon the following 182 morning the Midē′ priests, with the candidate in advance (No. 30), approach and enter the Midē′wigân and the initiation begins. No. 31 is the place of the sacred drum and those who are detailed to employ the drum and rattles, while No. 32 indicates the officiating priests; No. 33 is the degree post, surmounted by Kŏ-kŏ′-kŏ-ō′, the Owl (No. 34). The post is painted with vermilion, with small white spots all over its surface, emblematic of the mī′gis shell. The line (No. 35) extending along the upper portion of the inclosure represents the pole from which are suspended the robes, blankets, kettles, etc., which constitute the fee paid to the society for admission.

This degree is presided over and guarded by the Panther Man′idō.

When the candidate has been able to procure enough gifts to present to the society for the second degree, he takes his drum and offers chants (No. 35) to Ki′tshi Man′idō for success. Ki′tshi Man′idō himself is the guardian of the second degree and his footprints are shown in No. 36. No. 37 represents the second degree inclosure, and contains two sacred posts (Nos. 38 and 39), the first of which is the same as that of the first degree, the second being painted with white clay, bearing two bands of vermilion, one about the top and one near the middle. A small branch near the top is used, after the ceremony is over, to hang the tobacco pouch on. No. 40 represents the musicians and attendants; No. 41 the candidate upon his knees; while Nos. 42, 43, 44, and 45 pictures the officiating priests who surround him. The horizontal pole (No. 46) has presents of robes, blankets, and kettles suspended from it.

When a candidate is prepared to advance to the third degree (No. 47) he personates Makwa′ Man′idō, who is the guardian of this degree, and whose tracks (No. 48) are visible. The assistants are visible upon the interior, drumming and dancing. There are three sacred posts, the first (No. 49) is black, and upon this is placed Kŏ-ko′-kŏ-ō′— the Owl; the second (No. 50) is painted with white clay and has upon the top the effigy of an owl; while the third (No. 51) is painted with vermilion, bearing upon the summit the effigy of an Indian. Small wooden effigies of the human figure are used by the Midē′ in their tests of the proof of the genuineness and sacredness of their religion, which tests will be alluded to under another caption. The horizontal rod (No. 52), extending from one end of the structure to the other, has suspended from it the blankets and other gifts.

The guardian of the fourth degree is Maka′no—the Turtle—as he appears (No. 53) facing the entrance of the fourth degree (No. 54). Four sacred posts are planted in the fourth degree; the first (No. 55), being painted white upon the upper half and green upon the lower; the second (No. 56) similar; the third (No. 57) painted red, with a black spiral line extending from the top to the bottom, and upon which is placed Kŏ-ko′-kŏ-ō′—the Owl; and the fourth (No. 58), a cross, the arms and part of the trunk of which is white, with red spots—to designate the sacred mī′gis— the lower half of the trunk cut square, the face toward the east painted red, the south green, the west white, and the north black. The spot (No. 59) at the base of the cross signifies the place of the sacred stone, while the human figures (No. 60) designate the participants, some of whom are seated near the wall of the inclosure, whilst others are represented as beating the drum. Upon the horizontal pole (No. 61) are shown the blankets constituting gifts to the society.

facial decorations shown in color
Plate VII. Ojibwa Facial Decoration.

The several specific methods of facial decoration employed (Pl. VII), according to Ojibwa's statement, are as follows:

First degree.—One stripe of vermilion across the face, from near the ears across the tip of the nose.

Second degree.—One stripe as above, and another across the eyelids, temples, and the root of the nose.

183 *Third degree.*—The upper half of the face is painted green and the lower half red.

Fourth degree.—The forehead and left side of the face, from the outer canthus of the eye downward, is painted green; four spots of vermilion are made with the tip of the finger upon the forehead and four upon the green surface of the left cheek. In addition to this, the plumes of the golden eagle, painted red, are worn upon the head and down the back. This form of decoration is not absolutely necessary, as the expense of the "war bonnet" places it beyond the reach of the greater number of persons.

Before proceeding further with the explanation of the Midē′ records it may be of interest to quote the traditions relative to the migration of the Ani′shinâ′bēg, as obtained by Mr. Warren previous to 1853. In his reference to observing the rites of initiation he heard one of the officiating priests deliver "a loud and spirited harangue," of which the following words[12] caught his attention:

"Our forefathers were living on the great salt water toward the rising sun, the great Megis (seashell) showed itself above the surface of the great water and the rays of the sun for a long time period were reflected from its glossy back. It gave warmth and light to the An-ish-in-aub-ag (red race). All at once it sank into the deep, and for a time our ancestors were not blessed with its light. It rose to the surface and appeared again on the great river which drains the waters of the Great Lakes, and again for a long time it gave life to our forefathers and reflected back the rays of the sun. Again it disappeared from sight and it rose not till it appeared to the eyes of the An-ish-in-aub-ag on the shores of the first great lake. Again it sank from sight, and death daily visited the wigiwams of our forefathers till it showed its back and reflected the rays of the sun once more at Bow-e-ting (Sault Ste. Marie). Here it remained for a long time, but once more, and for the last time, it disappeared, and the An-ish-in-aub-ag was left in darkness and misery, till it floated and once more showed its bright back at Mo-ning-wun-a-kaun-ing (La Pointe Island), where it has ever since reflected back the rays of the sun and blessed our ancestors with life, light, and wisdom. Its rays reach the remotest village of the widespread Ojibways." As the old man delivered this talk he continued to display the shell, which he represented as an emblem of the great megis of which he was speaking.

A few days after, anxious to learn the true meaning of this allegory, *** I requested him to explain to me the meaning of his Me-da-we harangue.

After filling his pipe and smoking of the tobacco I had presented he proceeded to give me the desired information, as follows:

"My grandson," said he, "the megis I spoke of means the Me-da-we religion. Our forefathers, many string of lives ago, lived on the shores of the great salt water in the east. Here, while they were suffering the ravages of sickness and death, the Great Spirit, at the intercession of Man-a-bo-sho, the great common uncle of the An-ish-in-aub-ag, granted them this rite, wherewith life is restored and prolonged. Our forefathers moved from the shores of the great water and proceeded westward.

"The Me-da-we lodge was pulled down, and it was not again erected till our forefathers again took a stand on the shores of the great river where Mo-ne-aung (Montreal) now stands.

"In the course of time this town was again deserted, and our forefathers, still proceeding westward, lit not their fires till they reached the shores of Lake Huron, where again the rites of the Me-da-we were practiced.

"Again these rites were forgotten, and the Me-da-we lodge was not built till the Ojibways found themselves congregated at Bow-e-ting (outlet of Lake Superior), where it remained for many winters. Still the Ojibways moved westward, and for the last time the Me-da-we lodge was erected on the island of La Pointe, and here, long before the pale face appeared among them, it was practiced in its purest and most original form. Many of our fathers lived the full term of life granted to mankind by the Great Spirit, and the forms of many old people were mingled with each rising generation. This, my grandson, is the meaning of the words you did not understand; they have been repeated to us by our fathers for many generations."

In the explanation of the chart obtained at Red Lake, together with the tradition, reference to the otter, as being the most sacred emblem of society, is also verified in a brief notice of a tradition by Mr. Warren,13 as follows:

There is another tradition told by the old men of the Ojibway village of Fond du Lac, Lake Superior, which tells of their former residence on the shores of the great salt water. It is, however, so similar in character to the one I have related that its introduction here would only occupy unnecessary space. The only difference between the two traditions is that the otter, which is emblematical of one of the four Medicine Spirits who are believed to preside over the Midawe rites, is used in one in the same figurative manner as the seashell is used in the other, first appearing to the ancient An-ish-in-aub-ag from the depths of the great salt water, again on the river St. Lawrence, then on Lake Huron at Sault Ste. Marie, again at La Pointe, but lastly at Fond du Lac, or end of Lake Superior, where it is said to have forced the sand bank at the mouth of the St. Louis River. The place is still pointed out by the Indians where they believe the great otter broke through.

It is affirmed by the Indians that at Sault Ste. Marie some of the Ojibwa separated from the main body of that tribe and traversed the country along the northern shore of Lake Superior toward the west. These have since been known of as the "Bois Forts" (hardwood people or timber people), other bands being located at Pigeon River, Rainy Lake, etc. Another separation occurred at La Pointe, one party going toward Fond du Lac and westward to Red Lake, where they claim to have resided for more than three hundred years, while the remainder scattered from La Pointe westward and southwestward, locating at favorable places throughout the timbered country. This early dismemberment and long-continued separation of the Ojibwa nation accounts, to a considerable extent, for the several versions of the migration and the sacred emblems connected with the Midē´wiwin, the northern bands generally maintaining their faith in favor of the Otter as the guide, while the southern bodies are almost entirely supporters of the belief in the great mī´gis.

On account of the independent operations of the Midē´ priests in the various settlements of the Ojibwa, and especially because of the slight intercourse between those of the northern and southern divisions of the nation, there has arisen a difference in the pictographic representation of the same general ideas, variants which are frequently not recognized by Midē´ priests who are not members of the Midē´wiwin in which these mnemonic charts had their origin. As there are variants in the pictographic delineation of originally similar ideas, there are also corresponding variations in the traditions pertaining to them.

figure described in text

Fig. 6. —Birch-bark record, from White Earth.

The tradition relating to Mi´nabō´zho and the sacred objects received from Ki´tshi Man´idō for the Ani´shinâ´bēg is illustrated in Fig. 6, which is a reproduction of a chart preserved at White Earth. The record is read from left to right. No. 1 represents Mi´nabō´zho, who says of the adjoining characters representing the members of the Midē´wiwin: "They are the ones, they are the ones, who put into my heart the life." Mi´nabō´zho holds in his left hand the sacred Midē´ sack, or pin-ji´-gu-sân´. Nos. 2 and 3 represent the drummers. At the sound of the drum all the Midē´ rise and become inspired, because Ki´tshi Man´idō is then present in the wig´iwam. No. 4 denotes that women also have the privilege of becoming members of the Midē´wiwin. The figure holds in the left hand the Midē´ sack, made of a snake skin. No. 5 represents the Tortoise, the guardian spirit who was the giver of some of the sacred objects used in the rite. No. 6, the Bear, also a benevolent Man´idō, but not held in so great veneration as the Tortoise. His tracks are visible in the Midē´wiwin. No. 7, the sacred Midē´ sack or pin-ji´-gu-sân´, which contains life, and can be used by the Midē´ to prolong the life of a sick person. No. 8 represents a Dog, given by the Midē´ Man´idōs to Mi´nabō´zho as a companion.

Such was the interpretation given by the owner of the chart, but the informant was unconsciously in error, as has been ascertained not only from other Midē´ priests consulted with regard to the true meaning, but also in the light of later information and research in the exemplification of the ritual of the Midē´wiwin.

Mi´nabō´zho did not receive the rite from any Midē´ priests (Nos. 2 and 5), but from Ki´tshi Man´idō. Women are not mentioned in any of the earlier traditions of the origin of the society, neither was the dog given to Mi´nabō´zho, but Mi´nabō´zho gave it to the Ani´shinâ´bēg.

The chart, therefore, turns out to be a mnemonic song similar to others to be noted hereafter, and the owner probably copied it from 186 a chart in the possession of a stranger Midē´, and failed to learn its true signification, simply desiring it to add to his collection of sacred objects and to gain additional respect from his confrères and admirers.

figure described in text
    Fig. 7. —Birch-bark record, from Red Lake.

figure described in text
    Fig. 8. —Birch-bark record, from Red Lake.

Two similar and extremely old birch-bark mnemonic songs were found in the possession of a Midē´ at Red Lake. The characters upon these are almost identical, one appearing to be a copy of the other. These are reproduced in Figs. 7 and 8 . By some of the Midē´ Esh´gibō´-ga takes the place of Mi´nabō´zho as having originally received the Midē´wiwin from Ki´tshi Man´idō, but it is believed that the word is a synonym or a substitute based upon some reason to them inexplicable. These figures were obtained in 1887, and a brief explanation of them given in the American Anthropologist.14 At that time I could obtain but little direct information from the owners of the records, but it has since been ascertained that both are mnemonic songs pertaining to Mi´nabō´zho, or rather Eshgibō´ga, and do not form a part of the sacred records of the Midē´wiwin, but simply the pictographic representation of the possibilities and powers of the alleged religion. The following explanation of Figs. 7 and 8 is reproduced from the work just cited. A few annotations and corrections are added. The numbers apply equally to both illustrations:

No. 1, represents Esh´gibō´ga, the great uncle of the Ani´shinâ´bēg, and receiver of the Midē´wiwin.

No. 2, the drum and drumsticks used by Esh´gibō´ga.

No. 3, a bar or rest, denoting an interval of time before the song is resumed.

No. 4, the pin-ji´-gu-sân´ or sacred Midē´ sack. It consists of an otter skin, and is the mī´gis or sacred symbol of the Midē´wigân.

No. 5. a Midē´ priest, the one who holds the mī´gis while chanting the Midē´ song in the Midē´wigân. He is inspired, as indicated by the line extending from the heart to the mouth.

187 No. 6, denotes that No. 5 is a member of the Midē´wiwin. This character, with the slight addition of lines extending upward from the straight top line, is usually employed by the more southern Ojibwa to denote the wig´iwam of a Jĕss´akkīd´, or jugglery.

No. 7, is a woman, and signifies that women may also be admitted to the Midē´wiwin.

No. 8, a pause or rest.

No. 9, a snake-skin pin-ji´-gu-sân´ possessing the power of giving life. This power is indicated by the lines radiating from the head, and the back of the skin.

No. 10, represents a woman.

No. 11, is another illustration of the mī´gis, or otter.

No. 12, denotes a priestess who is inspired, as shown by the line extending from the heart to the mouth in Fig. 7 and simply showing the heart in Fig. 6 In the latter she is also empowered to cure with magic plants.

No. 13, in Fig. 7 , although representing a Midē´ priest, no explanation was given.

figure described in text
    Fig. 9. — Esh´gibō´ga.

Fig 9 is presented as a variant of the characters shown in No. 1 of Figs. 7 and 8 . The fact that this denotes the power of curing by the use of magic plants would appear to indicate an older and more appropriate form than the delineation of the bow and arrows, as well as being more in keeping with the general rendering of the tradition.

MIDĒ´WIGÂN.

Initiation into the Midē´wiwin or Midē´ Society is, at this time, performed during the latter part of summer. The ceremonies are performed in public, as the structure in which they are conducted is often loosely constructed of poles with intertwined branches and leaves, leaving the top almost entirely exposed, so that there is no difficulty in observing what may transpire within. Furthermore, the ritual is unintelligible to the uninitiated, and the important part of the necessary information is given to the candidate in a preceptor's wig´iwam.

To present intelligibly a description of the ceremonial of initiation as it occurred at White Earth, Minnesota, it will be necessary to first describe the structure in which it occurs, as well as the sweat lodge with which the candidate has also to do.

midewigan as described in text
Fig. 10. —
Diagram of Midē′wigân of the first degree.

The Midē′wigân, i.e., Midē′wig′iwam, or, as it is generally designated "Grand Medicine Lodge," is usually built in an open grove or clearing; it is a structure measuring about 80 feet in length by 20 in width, extending east and west with the main entrance toward that point of the compass at which the sun rises. The walls consist of poles and saplings from 8 to 10 feet high, firmly planted in the ground, wattled with short branches and twigs with leaves. In the east and west walls are left open spaces, each about 4 feet wide, 188 used as entrances to the inclosure. From each side of the opening the wall-like structure extends at right angles to the end wall, appearing like a short hallway leading to the inclosure, and resembles double doors opened outward. Fig. 10 represents a ground plan of the Midē′wigân, while Fig. 11 shows an interior view. Saplings thrown across the top of the structure serve as rafters, upon which are laid branches with leaves, and pieces of bark, to sufficiently shade the occupants from the rays of the sun. Several saplings extend across the inclosure near the top, while a few are attached to these so as to extend longitudinally, from either side of which presents of blankets, etc., may be suspended. About 10 feet from the main entrance a large flattened stone, measuring more than a foot in diameter, is placed upon the ground. This is used when subjecting to treatment a patient; and at a corresponding distance from the western door is planted the sacred Midē′ post of cedar, that for the first degree being about 7 feet in height and 6 or 8 inches in diameter. It is painted red, with a band of green 4 inches wide around the top. Upon the post is fixed the stuffed body of an owl. Upon that part of the floor midway between the stone and the Midē′ post is spread a blanket, upon which the gifts and presents to the society are afterward deposited. A short distance from each of the outer angles of the structure are planted cedar or pine trees, each about 10 feet in height.

midewigan interior
Fig. 11. —Interior of Midē′wigân.

189 About a hundred yards east of the main entrance is constructed a wig′iwam or sweat lodge, to be used by the candidate, both to take his vapor baths and to receive final instructions from his preceptor.

This wig′iwam is dome-shaped measures about 10 feet in diameter and 6 feet high in the middle, with an opening at the top which can be readily covered with a piece of bark. The framework of the structure consists of saplings stuck into the ground, the tops being bent over to meet others from the opposite side. Other thin saplings are then lashed horizontally to the upright ones so as to appear like hoops, decreasing in size as the summit is reached. They are secured by using strands of basswood bark. The whole is then covered with pieces of birchbark—frequently the bark of the pine is used—leaving a narrow opening on the side facing the Midē′wigân, which may be closed with an adjustable flap of bark or blankets.

The space between the Midē′wigân and the sweat lodge must be kept clear of other temporary shelters, which might be placed there by some of the numerous visitors attending the ceremonies.

FIRST DEGREE.

PREPARATORY INSTRUCTION.

When the candidate's application for reception into the Midē′wiwin has been received by one of the officiating priests, he calls upon the three assisting Midē′, inviting them to visit him at his own wig′iwam at a specified time. When the conference takes place, tobacco, which has been previously furnished by the candidate, is distributed and a smoke offering made to Ki′tshi Man′idō, to propitiate his favor in the deliberations about to be undertaken. The host then explains the object of the meeting, and presents to his auditors an account of the candidate's previous life; he recounts the circumstances of his fast and dreams, and if the candidate is to take the place of a lately deceased son who had been prepared to receive the degree, the fact is mentioned, as under such circumstances the forms would be different from the ordinary method of reception into the society. The subject of presents and gifts to the individual members of the society, as well as those intended to be given as a fee to the officiating priests, is also discussed; and lastly, if all things are favorable to the applicant, the selection of an instructor or preceptor is made, this person being usually appointed from among these four priests.

When the conference is ended the favorable decision is announced to the applicant, who acknowledges his pleasure by remitting to each of the four priests gifts of tobacco. He is told what instructor would be most acceptable to them, when he repairs to the wig′iwam of the person designated and informs him of his wish and the decision of the Midē′ council.

The designated preceptor arranges with his pupil to have certain days upon which the latter is to call and receive instruction and acquire 190 information. The question of remuneration being settled, tobacco is furnished at each sitting, as the Midē′ never begins his lecture until after having made a smoke-offering, which is done by taking a whiff and pointing the stem to the east; then a whiff, directing the stem to the south; another whiff, directing the stem to the west; then a whiff and a similar gesture with the stem to the north; another whiff is taken slowly and with an expression of reverence, when the stem is pointed forward and upward as an offering to Ki′tshi Man′idō; and finally, after taking a similar whiff, the stem is pointed forward and downward toward the earth as an offering to Nokō′mis, the grandmother of the universe, and to those who have passed before. After these preliminaries, the candidate receives at each meeting only a small amount of information, because the longer the instruction is continued daring the season before the meeting at which it is hoped the candidate may be admitted the greater will be the fees; and also, in order that the instruction may be looked upon with awe and reverence, most of the information imparted is frequently a mere repetition, the ideas being clothed in ambiguous phraseology. The Midē′ drum (Fig. 12 *a*) differs from the drum commonly used in dances (Fig. 12 *b*) in the fact that it is cylindrical, consisting of an elongated kettle or wooden vessel, or perhaps a section of the hollow trunk of a tree about 10 inches in diameter and from 18 to 20 inches in length, over both ends of which rawhide is stretched while wet, so that upon drying the membrane becomes hard and tense, producing, when beaten, a very hard, loud tone, which may be heard at a great distance.

drums

Fig. 12. —Ojibwa drums.

Frequently, however, water is put into the bottom of the drum and the drumhead stretched across the top in a wet state, which appears to intensify the sound very considerably.

The peculiar and special properties of the drum are described to the applicant; that it was at first the gift of Ki′tshi Man′idō, who gave it through the intercession of Mi′nabō′zho; that it is used to invoke the presence of the Midē′ Man′idōs, or sacred spirits, when seeking 191 direction as to information desired, success, etc.; that it is to be employed at the side of the sick to assist in the expulsion or exorcism of evil man′idōs who may possess the body of the sufferer; and that it is to be used in the. Midē′wigân during the initiation of new members or the advancement of a Midē′ from a degree to a higher one.

rattle   rattle
Fig. 13. —   Fig. 14. —
Midē′ rattle.   Midē′ rattle.

The properties of the rattle are next enumerated and recounted, its origin is related, and its uses explained. It is used at the side of a patient and has even more power in the expulsion of evil demons than the drum. The rattle is also employed in some of the sacred songs as an accompaniment, to accentuate certain notes and words. There are two forms used, one consisting of a cylindrical tin box filled with grains of corn or other seeds (Fig 13), the other being a hollow gourd also filled with seed (Fig. 14). In both of these the handle passes entirely through the rattle case.

In a similar manner the remaining gifts of Mi′nabō′zho are instanced and their properties extolled.

The mī′gis, a small white shell (Cypræa moneta L.) is next extracted from the Midē′ sack, or pinji′gusân′. This is explained as being the sacred emblem of the Midē′wiwin, the reason therefor being given in the account of the several traditions presented in connection with Pls. III , IV , and VIII . This information is submitted in parts, so that the narrative of the history connected with either of the records is extended over a period of time to suit the preceptor's plans and purposes. The ceremony of shooting the mī′gis (see Fig. 15) is explained on page 215.

figure described in text
Fig. 15. —Shooting the mī′gis.

As time progresses the preceptor instructs his pupil in Midē′ songs, i.e., he sings to him songs which form a part of his stock in trade, and which are alleged to be of service on special occasions, as when searching for medicinal plants, hunting, etc. The pupil thus acquires a comprehension of the method of preparing and reciting songs, which information is by him subsequently put to practical use in the composition and preparation of his own songs, the mnemonic characters employed being often rude copies of those observed upon the charts of his preceptor, but the arrangement thereof being original.

It is for this reason that a Midē′ is seldom, if ever, able to recite correctly any songs but his own, although he may be fully aware of the character of the record and the particular class of service in which it may be employed. In support of this assertion several songs obtained at Red Lake and imperfectly explained by "Little Frenchman" and "Leading Feather," are reproduced in Pl. XXII , A B , page 292.

192 From among the various songs given by my preceptor are selected and presented herewith those recognized by him as being part of the ritual. The greater number of songs are mere repetitions of short phrases, and frequently but single words, to which are added meaningless sounds or syllables to aid in prolonging the musical tones, and repeated ad libitum in direct proportion to the degree of inspiration in which the singer imagines himself to have attained. These frequent outbursts of singing are not based upon connected mnemonic songs preserved upon birch bark, but they consist of fragments or selections of songs which have been memorized, the selections relating to the subject upon which the preceptor has been discoursing, and which undoubtedly prompts a rythmic vocal equivalent. These songs are reproduced on Pl. IX , A, B, C . The initial mnemonic characters pertaining to each word or phrase of the original text are repeated below in regular order with translations in English, together with supplemental notes explanatory of the characters employed. The musical notation is not presented, as the singing consists of a monotonous repetition of four or five notes in a minor key; furthermore, a sufficiently clear idea of this may be formed by comparing some of the Midē′ songs presented in connection with the ritual of initiation and preparation of medicines. The first of the songs given herewith (Pl. IX , A) pertains to a request to Ki′tshi Man′idō that clear weather may be had for the 193 day of ceremonial, and also an affirmation to the candidate that the singer's words are a faithful rendering of his creed.

Each of the phrases is repeated before advancing to the next, as often as the singer desires and in proportion to the amount of reverence and awe with which he wishes to impress his hearer. There is usually a brief interval between each of the phrases, and a longer one at the appearance of a vertical line, denoting a rest, or pause. One song may occupy, therefore, from fifteen minutes to half an hour.

mnemonic song
Plate IX.a. Mnemonic Song.

line drawing Kí-we-na-wi´-´in mani´-i-dō´-ye-win.

I rock you, you that are a spirit.

[A midē's head, the lines denoting voice or speech—i.e., singing of sacred things, as the loops or circles at the ends of each line indicate.]

line drawing Kí-zhĭk-ki-wĭn´-da-mūn´.

The sky I tell you.

[The otter skin medicine sack, and arm reaching to procure something therefrom.]

line drawing O-we-nen´; hwīn´.

Who is it, who?

The mī´gis shell; the sacred emblem of the Midē´wiwin.

line drawing Wi´-dzhĭ-i-nan´.

The man helping me.

A man walking, the Midē´ Man´idō or Sacred Spirit.

line drawing Nu-wug´-ni-ma´na nin-guĭs´?

Have I told the truth to my son?

The bear going to the Midē´wigan and takes with him life to the Ani´shinâ´bēg.

vertical lines Rest.

line drawing Nĭn-dē´, ĕ´, ō´, ya´.

My heart, I am there (in the fullness of my heart).

My heart; knows all Midē´ secrets, sensible one.

194 A´-ni-na´-nĕsh-mi´-ĭ-an ni´-na´-wĭ-tō´.

line drawing I follow with my arms.

Arms extended to take up "medicine" or Midē´ secrets.

line drawing Man´-i-dō´-wi-an´ nĭ-me-shine´-mi´-an.

Knowledge comes from the heart, the heart reaches to sources of "medicine" in the earth.

[A Midē´ whose heart's desires and knowledge extend to the secrets of the earth. The lines diverging toward the earth denote direction.]

line drawing We´-gi-kwō´ Kĕ-mī´-nī-nan´?

From whence comes the rain? The power of making a clear sky, i.e., weather.

line drawing Mi-shŏk´ kwōt´, dzhe-man´-i-dō´-yan.

The sky, nevertheless, may be clear, Good Spirit.

Giving life to the sick; Dzhe Man´idō handing it to the Midē´.

line drawing Wi-ka-nŭn´-ĕ-nan.

Very seldom I make this request of you.

The Good Spirit filling the body of the supplicant with knowledge of secrets of the earth.

In the following song (Pl. IX , B), the singer relates to the candidate the gratitude which he experiences for the favors derived from the Good Spirit; he has been blessed with knowledge of plants and other sacred objects taken from the ground, which knowledge has been derived by his having himself become a member of the Midē´wiwin, and hence urges upon the candidate the great need of his also continuing in the course which he has thus far pursued.

mnemonic song
Plate IX.b. Mnemonic Song.

line drawing Nu-witsh´-tshi na-kŭm´-i-en a-na´-pi-a´?

When I am out of hearing, where am I?

The lines extending from the ears denote hearing; the arms directed toward the right and left, being the gesture of negation, usually made by throwing the hands outward and away from the front of the body.

line We´-nen-ne´ en´-da-yan.
drawing In my house, I see.

Sight is indicated by the lines extending from the eyes; the horns denote superiority of the singer.

195 Mo-kī´-yan-na´-a-witsh´-i-gūm´-mi.

When I rise it gives me life, and I take it.

line drawing

The arm reaches into the sky to receive the gifts which are handed down by the Good Spirit. The short transverse line across the forearm indicates the arch of the sky, this line being an abbreviation of the curve usually employed to designate the same idea.

line drawing Wen´-dzhi-ba´-pi-a´.

The reason why I am happy.

Asking the Spirit for life, which is granted. The singer's body is filled with the heart enlarged, i.e., fullness of heart, the lines from the mouth denoting abundance of voice or grateful utterances—singing.

Rest.

line drawing Zha´-zha-buí´-ki-bi-nan´ wig´-ĕ-wâm´.

The Spirit says there is plenty of "medicine" in the Midē´ wig´iwam.

[Two superior spirits, Ki´tshi Man´idō and Dzhe Man´idō, whose bodies are surrounded by "lines of sacredness," tell the Midē´ where the mysterious remedies are to be found. The vertical waving lines are the lines indicating these communications; the horizontal line, at the bottom, is the earth's surface.]

line Ya-hō´-hon-ni´-yŏ.
drawing The Spirit placed medicine in the ground, let us take it.

The arm of Ki´tshi Man´idō put into the ground sacred plants, etc., indicated by the spots at different horizons in the earth. The short vertical and waving lines denote sacredness of the objects.

line drawing Nu-wing-we-nī´-nan ki´-bi-do-na´.

I am holding this that I bring to you.

The singer sits in the Midē´wiwin, and offers the privilege of entrance, by initiation, to the hearer.

line drawing Mid́ī́gnĭ-kaʹ-năk kishʹ-o-wĕʹ-ni-mĭʹ-koʹ.

I have found favor in the eyes of my midēʹ friends.

The Good Spirit has put life into the body of the singer, as indicated by the two mysterious arms reaching towards his body, i.e., the heart, the seat of life.

In the following song (Pl. IX , C), the preceptor appears to feel satisfied that the candidate is prepared to receive the initiation, and therefore tells him that the Midēʹ Manʹidō announces to him the assurance. The preceptor therefore encourages his pupil with promises of the fulfillment of his highest desires.

mnemonic song
Plate IX.c. Mnemonic Song.

196 Baʹ-dzhĭ-keʹ-o giʹ-mand ma-bisʹ-in-dâʹ-ă.

line drawing I hear the spirit speaking to us.

The Midēʹ singer is of superior power, as designated by the horns and apex upon his head. The lines from the ears indicate hearing.

line drawing Kawīgäkʹ-in dīʹ-sha in-dâʹ-ya.

I am going into the medicine lodge.

The Midēʹwigân is shown with a line through it to signify that he is going through it, as in the initiation.

line drawing Kweʹ-tshĭ-ko-waʹ-ya tiʹ-na-man.

I am taking (gathering) medicine to make me live.

The discs indicate sacred objects within reach of the speaker.

line drawing Dī-wiŋyoʹ-in enʹ-do-ma mâkʹ-kwin-ĕnʹ-do-maʹ.

I give you medicine, and a lodge, also.

The Midēʹ, as the personator of Makwaʹ Manʹidō, is empowered to offer this privilege to the candidate.

line drawing Pī-winʹgnen bĕ-mīʹ-sĕt.

I am flying into my lodge.
Represents the Thunder-Bird, a deity flying into the arch of the sky. The short lines denote the (so-called spirit lines) abode of spirits or Manʹidōs.

line drawing Nawī-ne kwe-wēʹ-an.

The Spirit has dropped medicine from the sky where we can get it.

The line from the sky, diverging to various points, indicates that the sacred objects occur in scattered places.

line drawing Hāʹ-iŋg, ēʹ, ēʹ.

I have the medicine in my heart.

The singer's body—i.e., heart—is filled with knowledge relating to sacred medicines from the earth.

197

MIDĒʹ THERAPEUTICS.

During the period of time in which the candidate is instructed in the foregoing traditions, myths, and songs the subject of Midēʹ plants is also discussed. The information pertaining to the identification and preparation of the various vegetable substances is not imparted in regular order, only one plant or preparation, or perhaps two, being enlarged upon at a specified consultation. It may be that the candidate is taken into the woods where it is known that a specified plant or tree may be found, when a smoke offering is made before the object is pulled out of the soil, and a small pinch of tobacco put into the hole in the ground from which it was taken. This is an offering to Nokoʹmis—the earth, the grandmother of mankind—for the benefits which are derived from her body where they were placed by Kiʹtshi Manʹidō.

In the following list are presented, as far as practicable, the botanical and common names of these, there being a few instances in which the plants were not to be had, as they were foreign to that portion of Minnesota in which the investigations were made; a few of them, also, were not identified by the preceptors, as they were out of season.

It is interesting to note in this list the number of infusions and decoctions which are, from a medical and scientific standpoint, specific remedies for the complaints for which they are recommended. It is probable that the long continued intercourse between the Ojibwa and the Catholic Fathers, who were tolerably well versed in the ruder forms of medication, had much to do with improving an older and purely aboriginal form of practicing medical magic. In some of the remedies mentioned below there may appear to be philosophic reasons for their administration, but upon closer investigation it has been learned that the cure is not attributed to a regulation or restoration of functional derangement, but to the removal or even expulsion of malevolent beings—commonly designated as bad Manʹidōs—supposed to have taken possession of that part of the body in which such derangement appears most conspicuous. Further reference to the mythic properties of some of the plants employed will be made at the proper time.

Although the word Mashki kiwaʹbu—medicine broth—signifies liquid medical preparations, the term is usually employed in a general sense to pertain to the entire materia medica; and in addition to the alleged medicinal virtues extolled by the preceptors, certain parts of the trees and plants enumerated are eaten on account of some mythic reason, or employed in the construction or manufacture of habitations, utensils, and weapons, because of some supposed supernatural origin or property, an explanation of which they have forgotten.

198

Pinus strobus, L. White Pine. Zhing-wâkʹ.

1. The leaves are crushed and applied to relieve headache; also boiled; after which they are put into a small hole in the ground and hot stones placed therein to cause a vapor to ascend, which is inhaled to cure backache.

The fumes of the leaves heated upon a stone or a hot iron pan are inhaled to cure headache.

2. Gum; chiefly used to cover seams of birch-bark canoes. The gum is obtained by cutting a circular band of bark from the trunk, upon which it is then

scraped and boiled down to proper consistence. The boiling was formerly done in clay vessels.

Pinus resinosa, Ait. Red Pine; usually, though erroneously, termed Norway Pine. Pŏkgwĕ′nagē′mŏk.

Used as the preceding.

Abies balsamea, Marshall. Balsam Fir. Ini′nandŏk.

1. The bark is scraped from the trunk and a decoction thereof is used to induce diaphoresis.

2. The gum, which is obtained from the vesicles upon the bark, and also by skimming it from the surface of the water in which the crushed bark is boiled, is carried in small vessels and taken internally as a remedy for gonorrhoea and for soreness of the chest resulting from colds.

3. Applied externally to sores and cuts.

Abies alba, Michx. White Spruce. Sĕ′ssēgân′dŏk. The split roots—wadŏb′-are used for sewing; the wood for the inside timbers of canoes.

Abies nigra, Poir. Black Spruce. A′mikwan′dŏk.

1. The leaves and crushed bark are used to make a decoction, and sometimes taken as a substitute in the absence of pines.

2. Wood used in manufacture of spear handles.

Abies Canadensis, Michx. Hemlock. Saga′īwush—"Raven Tree."

Outer bark powdered and crushed and taken internally for the cure of diarrhea. Usually mixed with other plants not named.

Larix Americana, Michx. Tamarack. Mŏsh′kīkiwa′dik.

1. Crushed leaves and bark used as Pinus strobus.

2. Gum used in mending boats.

3. Bark used for covering wig′iwams.

Cupressus thyoides, L. White Cedar. Gi′zhĭk—"Day."

1. Leaves crushed and used as Pinus strobus. The greater the variety of leaves of coniferæ the better. The spines of the leaves exert their prickly influence through the vapor upon the demons possessing the patient's body.

2. The timber in various forms is used in the construction of canoe and lodge frames, the bark being frequently employed in roofing habitations.

Juniperus Virginiana, L. Red Cedar. Muskwa′wâ′ak.

Bruised leaves and berries are used internally to remove headache.

Quercus alba, L. White Oak. Mītig′ōmish′.

1. The bark of the root and the inner bark scraped from the trunk is boiled and the decoction used internally for diarrhea.

2. Acorns eaten raw by children, and boiled or dried by adults.

Quercus rubra, L. Red Oak. Wisug-′emītig′omish′—"Bitter Acorn Tree."

Has been used as a substitute for Q. alba.

Acer saccharinum, Wang. Sugar Maple. Innīnâ′tik.

1. Decoction of the inner bark is used for diarrhea.

2. The sap boiled in making sirup and sugar.

3. The wood valued for making arrow shafts.

199

Acer nigrum, Michx. Black Sugar Maple. Ishig′omeaush′— "Sap-flows-fast."

Arbor liquore abundans, ex quo liquor tanquam urina vehementer projicitur.

Sometimes used as the preceding.

Betula excelsa, Ait. Yellow Birch. Wi′umis′sik.

The inner bark is scraped off, mixed with that of the Acer saccharinum, and the decoction taken as a diuretic.

Betula papyracea, Ait. White Birch. Mīgwas′.

Highly esteemed, and employed for making records, canoes, syrup-pans, mōkoks′—or sugar boxes—etc. The record of the Midē′wiwin, given by Minabō′zho, was drawn upon this kind of bark.

Populus monilifera, Ait. Cottonwood. Mâ′nâsâ′ti.

The cotton down is applied to open sores as an absorbent.

Populus balsamifera, L. Balsam Poplar. Asa′dī.

1. The bark is peeled from the branches and the gum collected and eaten.

2. Poles are used in building ordinary shelter lodges, and particularly for the Midē′wigân.

Juglans nigra, L. Black Walnut. Paga′nŏk—"Nut wood."

Walnuts are highly prized; the green rind of the unripe fruit is sometimes employed in staining or dyeing.

Smilacina racemosa, Desf. False Spikenard. Kinē′wigwŏshk—"Snake weed or Snake Vine."

1. Warm decoction of leaves used by lying-in women.

2. The roots are placed upon a red-hot stone, the patient, with a blanket thrown over his head, inhaling the fumes, to relieve headache.

3. Fresh leaves are crushed and applied to cuts to stop bleeding.

Helianthus occidentalis, Riddell. Sunflower. Pŭkite′wŭkbŏkus′.

The crushed root is applied to bruises and contusions.

Polygala senega, L. Seneca Snakeroot. Winis′sikēs′.

1. A decoction of the roots is used for colds and cough.

2. An infusion of the leaves is given for sore throat; also to destroy waterbugs that have been swallowed.

Rubus occidentalis, L. Black Raspberry. Makadē′wĭskwi′minŏk—"Black Blood Berry."

A decoction made of the crushed roots is taken to relieve pains in the stomach.

Rubus strigosus, Michx. Wild Red Raspberry. Miskwi′minŏk′—"Blood Berry."

The roots are sometimes used as a substitute for the preceding.

Gaylussacia resinosa, Torr. and Gr. Huckleberry. Mī′nŭn.

Forms one of the chief articles of trade during the summer. The berry occupies a conspicuous place in the myth of the "Road of the Dead," referred to in connection with the "Ghost Society."

Prunus Virginiana, L. Choke Cherry. Sisa′wewi′nakâsh′.

1. The branchlets are used for making an ordinary drink; used also during gestation.

2. The fruit is eaten.

Prunus serotina, Ehrhart. Wild Black Cherry. Okwē′wĭsh—"Scabby Bark."

1. The inner bark is applied to external sores, either by first boiling, bruising, or chewing it.

2. An infusion of the inner bark is sometimes given to relieve pains and soreness of the chest.

Prunus Pennsylvanica, L. Wild Red Cherry. Kusigwa′kumĭ′nŏk.

1. A decoction of the crushed root is given for pains and other stomach disorders.

2. Fruit is eaten and highly prized.

3. This, believed to be synonymous with the June Cherry of Minnesota, is referred to in the myths and ceremonies of the "Ghost Society."

200

Prunus Americana, Marsh. Wild Plum. Bogē′sanŏk.

The small rootlets, and the bark of the larger ones, are crushed and boiled together with the roots of the following named plants, as a remedy for diarrhea. The remaining plants were not in bloom at the time during which the investigations were made, and therefore were not identified by the preceptors, they being enabled to furnish only the names and an imperfect description. They are as follows, viz: Minē′sŏk, two species, one with red berries, the other with yellow ones; Wabō′saminī′sŏk—"Rabbit berries"; Shi′gwanau′isŏk, having small red berries; and Cratægus coccinea, L. Scarlet-fruited Thorn. O′ginīk.

Typha latifolia, L. Common Cat-tail. Napŏgŭshk—"Flat grass."

The roots are crushed by pounding or chewing, and applied as a poultice to sores.

Sporobolus heterolepis Gr. Napŏ′gŭshkūs′—"Little Flat Grass."

1. Used sometimes as a substitute for the preceding.

2. Roots are boiled and the decoction taken to induce emesis, "to remove bile."

Fragaria vesca, L. Wild Strawberry. Odē ĭmĭn′nĕ—Heart Berry.

Referred to in the ceremony of the "Ghost Society."

The fruit is highly valued as a luxury.

Acer Pennsylvanicum, L. Striped Maple. Mō′zomīsh′—"Moose Wood." The inner bark scraped from four sticks or branches, each two feet long, is put into a cloth and boiled, the liquid which can subsequently be pressed out of the bag is swallowed, to act as an emetic.

Fraxinus sambucifolia, Lam. Black or Water Ash. A′gimak′.

1. The inner bark is soaked in warm water, and the liquid applied to sore eyes.

2. The wood is employed in making the rims for frames of snow-shoes.

Veronica Virginica, L. Culver's Root. Wi′sōgedzhi′wĭk—"Bitter Root."

A decoction of the crushed root is taken as a purgative.

Salix Candida, Willd. Hoary Willow. Sisi′gewe′mĭsh.

The thick inner bark of the roots is scraped off, boiled, and the decoction taken for cough

Symphoricarpus vulgaris, Michx. Indian Currant. Gus′sigwaka′mĭsh.

The inner bark of the root boiled and the decoction, when cold, applied to sore eyes.

Geum strictum, Ait. Aven. Ne′bone′ankwe′âk—" Hair on one side."

The roots are boiled and a weak decoction taken internally for soreness in the chest, and cough.

Rumex crispus, L. Curled Dock. O′zabetshi′wĭk.

The roots are bruised or crushed and applied to abrasions, sores, etc.

Amorpha canescens, Nutt. Lead Plant. We′abŏnag′kak—"That which turns white."

A decoction made of the roots, is used for pains in the stomach. *Rosa blanda*, Ait. Early Wild Rose. O′ginīk.

A piece of root placed in lukewarm water, after which the liquid is applied to inflamed eyes.

Anemone (sp.?) Anemone. Wisōg′ibŏk′; also called Hartshorn plant by the mixed-bloods of Minnesota.

The dry leaves are powdered and used as an errhine, for the cure of headache.

(Gen. et sp. ?) Termed Kine′bĭk wash′kos and "Snake weed."

This plant was unfortunately so injured in transportation that identification was impossible. Ball-players and hunters use it to give them endurance and speed; the root is chewed when necessary to possess these qualities. The root is likened to a snake, which is supposed to be swift in motion and possessed of extraordinary muscular strength.

201

Rhus (*aromatica*, Ait. ?) "White Sumac." Bŏkkwan′ībŏk.

Roots are boiled, with those of the following named plant, and the decoction taken to cure diarrhea.

(*Gen. et sp. ?*) Ki′tshiodēiminibŏk—"Big Heart Leaf."

Roots boiled, with preceding, and decoction taken for diarrhea.

Monarda fistulosa, L. Wild Bergamot. Moshkōs′waowis′—"Little Elk's Tail."

The root is used by making a decoction and drinking several swallows, at intervals, for pain in the stomach and intestines.

Hydrophyllum Virginicum, L. Waterleaf. Hukite′wagūŭs′.

The roots are boiled, the liquor then taken for pains in the chest, back, etc.

Anemone Pennsylvanicum, L. Pennsylvania Anemone. Pesī′kwadzhi′bwiko′kŏk.

A decoction of the roots is used for pains in the lumbar region.

Viola (*Canadensis*, L.?). Canada Violet. Maskwī′widzhī′wiko′kŏk.

The decoction made of the roots is used for pains in the region of the bladder.

Phryma leptostachya, L. Lopseed. Waia′bishkĕno′kŏk.

The roots are boiled and the decoction taken for rheumatic pains in the legs.

Viola pubescens, Ait. Downy Yellow Violet, Ogitē′wagus.

A decoction is made of the roots, of which small doses are taken at intervals for sore throat.

Rosa (*lucida*, Ehrhart?). Dwarf Wild Rose. Oginī′minaga′mŏs.

The roots of young plants are steeped

in hot water and the liquid applied to sore eyes.

(Gen. et sp. ?) Mŏ´zânâ´tĭk.

This plant could not be identified at the locality and time at which investigations were conducted. The root is boiled and the decoction taken as a diuretic for difficult micturition.

Actæa rubra, Michx. Red Baneberry. Odzī´bĭkĕs´—"Little Root."

A decoction of the root, which has a sweet taste, is used for stomachic pains caused by having swallowed hair (mythic). Used also in conjunction with Ginseng.

This plant, according to some peculiarities, is considered the male plant at certain seasons of the year, and is given only to men and boys, while the same plant at other seasons, because of size, color of fruit, or something else, is termed the female, and is prepared for women and girls in the following manner, viz: The roots are rolled in basswood leaves and baked, when they become black; an infusion is then prepared, and used in a similar manner as above.

The latter is called Wash´kubĭdzhi´bikakŏk´.

Botrychium Virginicum, Swartz. Moonwort. Ozaga´tigŭm.

The root is bruised and applied to cuts.

Aralia trifolia, Gr. Dwarf Ginseng. Nesō´wakŏk—"Three Leafed."

The roots are chewed and the mass applied to cuts to arrest hemorrhage.

Echinospermum lappula, Lehm. Stickweed. Ozaga´tĭgomĕs—"Burr Bush."

The roots are placed in a hole in the ground upon hot stones, to cause the fumes to rise, when the patient puts down his face and has a cloth or blanket thrown over his head. The fumes are inhaled for headache. The raw roots are also sniffed at for the same purpose.

It is affirmed by various members of the Midē´ Society that in former times much of the information relating to some of these plants was not imparted to a candidate for initiation into the first degree, but was reserved for succeeding degrees, to induce a Midē´ of the first degree to endeavor to attain higher distinction and further advancement in the mysteries of the order. As much knowledge is believed to have been lost through the reticence and obstinacy of former chief priests, the so-called higher secrets are now imparted at the first and second degree preparatory instructions. The third and fourth degrees are very rarely conferred, chiefly because the necessary presents and fees are beyond the reach of those who so desire advancement, and partly also because the missionaries, and in many instances the Indian agents, have done their utmost to suppress the ceremonies, because they were a direct opposition and hindrance to progress in Christianizing influences.

When the preparatory instruction has come to an end and the day of the ceremony of initiation is at hand, the preceptor sings to his pupil a song, expatiating upon his own efforts and the high virtue of the knowledge imparted. The pipe is brought forward and an offering of tobacco smoke made by both preceptor and pupil, after which the former sings a song (Pl. X , A .), the time of its utterance being tediously prolonged. The mnemonic characters were drawn by Sikas´sigĕ, and are a copy of an old birch-bark scroll which has for many years been in his possession, and which was made in imitation of one in the possession of his father, Baiĕ´dzĭk, one of the leading Midē´ at Mille Lacs, Minnesota.

mnemonic song
Plate X.a. Mnemonic Song.

line drawing Wĭ-ka-no´-shi-a-ŏ.
ing My arm is almost pulled out from digging medicine. It is full of medicine.

The short zigzag lines signifying magic influence, erroneously designated "medicine."

line We-wī´-ka-ni´-an.
drawing Almost crying because the medicine is lost.

The lines extending downward from the eye signifies weeping; the circle beneath the figure is the place where the "medicine" is supposed to exist. The idea of "lost" signifies that some information has been forgotten through death of those who possessed it.

line drawing Me-shi´-âk-kĭnk mi-sui´-a-kĭnk.
ing Yes, there is much medicine you may cry for.

Refers to that which is yet to be learned of.

line drawing Pe-wä-mĭ-ko-ya´-na-kĭnk´.
Yes, I see there is plenty of it.

The Midē´ has knowledge of more than he has imparted, but reserves that knowledge for a future time. The lines of "sight" run to various medicines which he perceives or knows of.

ver- Rest.
ti-
cal
lines

We´-a-kwĕ´-nĭnk pe-ĭ-e´-mi-wĭt´-o-wan´.
line When I come out the sky becomes clear.
drawing
 When the otter-skin Midē´ sack is produced the sky becomes clear, so that the ceremonies may proceed.

line drawing Wĭ-kwĕ-nĭnk´ ke´-tŏ-nĭnk´ e´-
ing to-wa´.

The spirit has given me power to see.

The Midē´ sits on a mountain the better to commune with the Good Spirit.

line drawing Mĭ-sha-kwat´-ni-yō´.
ing I brought the medicine to bring life.

The Midē´ Man´idō, the Thunderer, after bringing some of the plants—by causing the rains to fall—returns to the sky. The short line represents part of the circular line usually employed to designate the imaginary vault of the sky.

line drawing Me´-ka-yĕ´-nĭnk te´-a-yĕ-am´-
ing ban.

I, too, see how much there is.

His power elevates the Midē´ to the rank of a man´idō, from which point he perceives many

secrets hidden in the earth.
line draw- Ena-we´-be-mī´-ko.
ing I am going to the medicine lodge.

The vertical left-hand figure denotes a leg going toward the Midē´wigân.

line draw- In-de´-bi-bi´-to.
ing I take life from the sky.

The Midē´ is enabled to reach into the sky and to obtain from Ki´tshi Man´idō the means of prolonging life. The circle at the top denotes the sacred mī´gis, or shell.

line draw- Nowaṅgwi´-mi-kō´.
ing Let us talk to one another.

The circles denote the places of the speaker (Midē´) and the hearer (Ki´tshi Man´idō), the short lines signifying magic influences, the Midē´ occupying the left hand and smaller seat.

line draw- Man´-i-dō-ye-na´-ni ni-kan´.
ing The spirit is in my body, my friend.

The mī´gis, given by Ki´tshi Man´idō, is in contact with the Midē´'s body, and he is possessed of life and power.

From ten days to two weeks before the day of initiation, the chief Midē´ priest sends out to all the members invitations, which consist of sticks one-fourth of an inch thick and 6 or 7 inches long. The courier is charged with giving to the person invited explicit information as to the day of the ceremony and the locality where it is to 204 be held. Sometimes these sticks have bands of color painted around one end, usually green, sometimes red, though both colors may be employed, the two ends being thus tinted. The person invited is obliged to bring with him his invitation stick, and upon entering the Midē´wigân he lays it upon the ground near the sacred stone, on the side toward the degree post. In case a Midē´ is unable to attend he sends his invitation with a statement of the reason of his inability to come. The number of sticks upon the floor are counted, on the morning of the day of initiation, and the number of those present to attend the ceremonies is known before the initiation begins.

About five or six days preceding the day set for the ceremony of initiation, the candidate removes to the neighborhood of the locality of the Midē´wigân. On the evening of the fifth day he repairs to the sudatory or sweat-lodge, which has, in the meantime, been built east of the sacred inclosure, and when seated within he is supplied with water which he keeps for making vapor by pouring it upon heated stones introduced for the purpose by assistants upon the outside. This act of purification is absolutely necessary and must be performed once each day for four days, though the process may be shortened by taking two vapor baths in one day, thus limiting the process to two days. This, however, is permitted, or desired only under extraordinary circumstances. During the process of purgation, the candidates thoughts must dwell upon the seriousness of the course he is pursuing and the sacred character of the new life he is about to assume.

When the fumigation has ceased he is visited by the preceptor and the other officiating Midē´ priests, when the conversation is confined chiefly to the candidate's progress. He then gives to each of them presents of tobacco, and after an offering to Ki´tshi Man´idō, with the pipe, they expose the articles contained in their Midē´ sacks and explain and expatiate upon the merits and properties of each of the magic objects. The candidate for the first time learns of the manner of preparing effigies, etc., with which to present to the incredulous ocular demonstration of the genuineness and divine origin of the Midē´wiwin, or, as it is in this connection termed, religion.

Several methods are employed for the purpose, and the greater the power of the Midē´ the greater will appear the mystery connected with the exhibition. This may be performed whenever circumstances demand such proof, but the tests are made before the candidate with a twofold purpose: first, to impress him with the supernatural powers of the Midē´ themselves; and second, in an oracular manner, to ascertain if Ki´tshi Ma´nidō is pleased with the contemplated ceremony and the initiation of the candidate.
205

beads
Fig. 16.

The first test is made by laying upon the floor of the wig´iwam a string of four wooden beads each measuring about 1 inch in diameter. See Fig. 16. After the owner of this object has chanted for a few moments in an almost inaudible manner the beads begin to roll from side to side as if animated. The string is then quickly restored to its place in the Midē´ sack. Another Midē´ produces a small wooden effigy of a man (Fig. 17), measuring about 5 inches in height. The body has a small orifice running through it from between the shoulders to the buttocks, the head and neck forming a separate piece which may be attached to the body like a glass stopper to a bottle.

A hole is made in the ground deep enough to reach to the hips of the effigy, when the latter is put into it and the loose earth loosely restored so as to hold it in an upright position. Some magic powder of herbs is sprinkled around the body, and into the vertical orifice in 206 it, when the head is put in place. A series of inarticulate utterances are chanted, when, if everything be favorable, the figure will perceptibly move up and down as if possessed of life. Fig. 18 represents another figure used in a similar manner. It consists of one piece, however, and is decorated with narrow bands of dark blue flannel about the ankles and knees, a patch of red cloth upon the breast and bands about the wrists, each of the eyes being indicated by three white porcelain beads.

effigy effigy
Fig. 17. Fig. 18.

One of the most astonishing tests, however, and one that can be produced only by Midē´ of the highest power, consists in causing a Midē´ sack to move upon the ground as if it were alive. This, it is confidently alleged, has been done repeatedly, though it is evident that the deception is more easily produced than in the above-mentioned instances, as the temporary retention within a bag of a small mammal could readily be made to account for the movements.

In most of these private exhibitions the light is so obscured as to prevent the deception being observed and exposed; and when public demonstrations of skill are made the auditors invariably consist of the most credulous of the uninitiated, or the confréres of the performer, from whom no antagonism or doubt would be expected.

The preceptor then consults with the Midē´ priests respecting the presents to be delivered by the candidate, and repeats the following words, viz:

Mis-shai´-ĕ-gwa	tshi-dĕ-bŏg-in-de-mung´	gi´-she-gŏ-dung´
Now is the time	that we shall fix the price	of everything pertaining to the sky,
ka-mi´-nĕ-nŏngk gi´-she-goy-dŭng´		di´-bi-ga-dōnk´ gai-yé´.
that has been	given to us	from the day	[and]	the night also.
A-pē´-gĕ-dá´wŭnk	i´-wa-pī	ge-bin´-de-ga-yŏngk´,
When it shall come to pass	and at the time	that we shall enter,

ă-au´-wa-mi-dē´-wĭd.

he who wishes to become a Midē´.

When the four vapor baths have been taken by the candidate, and the eve of the ceremony has arrived, he remains in the sudatory longer than usual so as not to come in contact with the large crowd of visitors who have arrived upon the scene. The woods resound with the noises incident to a large camp, while in various directions may be heard the monotonous beating of the drum indicating the presence of a number of dancers, or the hard, sharp taps of the midē´ drum, caused by a priest propitiating and invoking the presence and favor of Ki´tshi Ma´nidō in the service now so near at hand.

When the night is far advanced and all becomes hushed, the candidate, with only the preceptor accompanying, retires to his own wig´iwam, while the assistant Midē´ priests and intimate friends or members of his family collect the numerous presents and suspend them from the transverse and longitudinal poles in the upper part of the Midē´wigân. Watchers remain to see that nothing is removed during the night.

At the approach of day, the candidate breakfasts and again returns to the sweat-lodge to await the coming of his preceptor, and, later, of the officiating priests. The candidate puts on his best clothing 207 and such articles of beaded ornaments as he may possess. The preceptor and Midē´ priests are also clad in their finest apparel, each wearing one or two beaded dancing bags at his side, secured by a band of beaded cloth crossing the opposite shoulder. The members of the Midē´wiwin who are not directly concerned in the preliminaries resort to the Midē´wigân and take seats around the interior, near the wall, where they may continue to smoke, or may occasionally drum and sing. The drummer, with his assistants, takes a place near upon the floor of the sacred inclosure to the left of the eastern entrance, i.e., the southeast corner.

IMPLORATION FOR CLEAR WEATHER.

Should the day open up with a threatening sky, one of the Midē´ priests accompanying the candidate sings the following song (Pl. X , B) to dispel the clouds. Each of the lines is repeated an indefinite number of times, and after being repeated once or twice is sung also by the others as an accompaniment.

It will be observed that the words as spoken vary to some extent when chanted or sung.

mnemonic song
Plate X.b. Mnemonic Song.
line Hi-dra-wēnghē´, ki´-ne-na-wē´ man´-i-dō.
 I swing the spirit like a child.
 The Midē´ Spirit, showing magic lines radiating from his body. The Midē´ claims to be able to receive special favor.

musical notation
 Ki´nana´wein, Ki´nana´wein, Ki´nana´wein, Man´ido´weēg;
 Ki´nana´wein, Ki´nana´wein, Ki´nana´wein, Man´ido´weēg´;
 Ki´nana´wein, Man´ido´weēg´.
 MIDI files: drum , flute , piano (default)
line Gi-zhik´-ē´ ka-hwē´ da-mū´-nĕ.
drawing The sky is what I am telling you about.
 The sky and the earth united by a pathway of possible rain.

musical notation
 Ki´zhiga´widâ´ mu´nedē´, Ki´zhiga´widâ´ mu´nedē´,
 Ki´zhiga´widâ´ Ki´zhi-ga´wi-dâ´,
 Ki´zhi-ga´wi-dâ mu´nedē´, Ki´zhiga´widâ mu´nedē´.
 MIDI files: drum , flute , piano (default)
208
line Wa-ne-o-ho ne´-ge-shi´-go-ni
drawing Ko-sa´-we, hē´, wa-ni´-sha´-na´.
ing We have lost the sky [it becomes dark].
 [Clouds obscure the sky, and the arm of the Midē´ is reaching up into it for its favor of clear weather.]
musical notation
 Waneo-ho hē ne´-ge-shi-go-ni, Wane-o-ho-hē ne´-ge-shi-go-ni,
 Ko´sawe ne hē wa´nishi-na-ha, waneo-ho-hē ne´-ge-shi-go-ni.
 MIDI files: drum , flute , piano (default)
line Ni-tshi´-hi-na´-ne-he, nē´, kō´, hō.
drawing nō´-ni-wi-tshi-nan´.
ing I am helping you.
 [The Otter-skin Midē´ sack is held up to influence the Otter Spirit to aid them.]
musical notation
 Wi´tshihinanehe nē´ kō hō´, ne´ni-wi´tshinan, wi´tshihinanehe
 nē´ kō´ hō´. U-a-ni-ma wē u-a-ni-ma wē henigwish.
 MIDI files: drum , flute , piano (default)
line He-a´-ni-ma´, wē´, he´-ni-gwĭsh.
drawing I have made an error [in sending].
ing The Otter-skin Midē´ sack has failed to produce the desired effect.

Rest.

vertical lines

The Midē´ women who have gathered without the lodge now begin to dance as the song is renewed.

line drawing Na-nin-dē´, hē´, he-yo-ya, nē´.
I am using my heart.
Refers to sincerity of motives in practice of Midē´ ceremony.

209 Yo´-na-hĭsh´-i-me´-a´-ne´, hē´. yá-na-hĭsh-a-me´-a-ne´, hē´.

line drawing What are you saying to me, and I am "in my senses"?

line drawing Man´-i-dō, hē´ nē´, mē´-de-wē´, nē´.
The spirit wolf.
One of the malevolent spirits who is opposed to having the ceremony is assisting the evil man´idōs in causing the sky to be overcast.

line drawing Wen´-tshi-o-ne-se hē´, nē´, wen´-tshi-o-ne-se hē´.
I do not know where I am going.
The Midē´ is in doubt whether to proceed or not in the performance of initiation.

line drawing Mi´-shok-kwo´-ti-ne be-wa´-ne, ni-bin´-zhi man´-i-dō i-ya´-nē.
I depend on the clear sky.
[To have the ceremony go on. Arm reaching toward the sky for help.]

line drawing Ke-me´-ni-na-ne´ a-nō´-ē´ ingsho-wē´ me-nō´-de ki-man´-i-dō.
I give you the other village, spirit that you are.
[That rain should fall anywhere but upon the assemblage and Midē´wigân.]

line drawing Tshing-gwē´-o-dē |: gē´.
The thunder is heavy.
The Thunder Bird, who causes the rain.

page image

line drawing Mi´-wi-ka-nō´, hō´ shi-a-dē´.
We are talking to one another.
The Midē´ communes with Ki´tshi Man´idō; he is shown near the sky; his horns denoting superior wisdom and power, while the lines from the mouth signify speech.

In case the appearance of the sky becomes sufficiently favorable the initiation begins, but if it should continue to be more unfavorable or to rain, then the song termed the "Rain Song" is resorted to and sung within the inclosure of the Midē´wigân, to which they all march in solemn procession. Those Midē´ priests who have with them their Midē´ drums use them as an accompaniment to the singing and to propitiate the good will of Ki´tshi Man´idō. Each line of the entire song appears as an independent song, the intervals of rest varying in time according to the feelings of the officiating priest.

The words of the song are known to most of the Midē´ priests; but, as there is no method of retaining a set form of musical notation, the result is entirely individual and may vary with each singer, if sung independently and out of hearing of others; so that, under 210 ordinary circumstances, the priest who leads off sings through one stanza of the song, after which the others will readily catch the notes and accompany him. It will be observed, also, that the words as spoken vary to some extent when chanted or sung.

If this song does not appear to bring about a favorable change the priests return to their respective wig´iwams and the crowd of visitors disperses to return upon the first clear day.

INITIATION OF CANDIDATE.

If, however, the day be clear and promising the candidate goes early to the sweat-lodge, where he is joined by his preceptor, and later by the officiating priest. After all preliminaries have been arranged and the proper time for regular proceedings has arrived, the preceptor sings the following song (Pl. X, C), the musical notation of which varies according to his feelings, clearly showing that there is no recognized method of vocal delivery, as is the case with the music of dancing songs:

mnemonic song
Plate X.c. Mnemonic Song.

line drawing Kaw-ing´-e-a-nē´, to´-e-a-nē´ kan-do´-e-a-nē´, in-nin´-nĭ man´-e-dō´-ē´.
The spirit man is crying out.
[The head of the Midē´, a synonym of Ki´tshi Man´idō. The voice lines show spots denoting intensity of accentuation, and that Ki´tshi Man´idō is pleased to look with favor upon the proceedings.]

line drawing Ya-wing-ē´, na´, tshi-mo-tē´, hē´.
Talking around in various sections.
The voice lines, as in the preceding figure, extending downward from the mouth to either side, have spots upon them to indicate "talks" in various directions addressed to the Midē´.

line drawing Man´-e-dō, wē´, hē´, pe-me´-so-wing´.
The spirit is flying.
The Thunder Bird, who causes the rain, is away at some remote place.

line drawing Mi-de´-we-tē-we´ me´-wa-gwi´-shak-wa´, mi-de´-we-ta´.
The day is clear; let us have the grand medicine.
[The Midē´'s hand reaches to the sky, and rain falls at places other than upon the Midē´wigân, as shown by rain lines from the end of the curved lines denoting the sky.]

line drawing Me-shak´-kwot dung´-ke-hē´, ne-mē´-gĭs-sīm´.
I am the sign that the day will be clear.
[The Midē´'s hand reaches to the sky, as indicated by the short transverse line, and the sun's rays diverge in all directions.]

211 Sun´-gis-ni de´-wit-ka-nē´, hē´, wi-no´-wo-he´-she-wat´ man´-i-do-wi-tshik.

line drawing I am the strongest medicine, is what is said of me.
[The speaker compares himself to Makwa´ Man´idō, the Bear Spirit.]

Hwo´-ba-mī´-de, hwo´-ba-mī-

line drawing
de, man-ĕ-dō na´-wa-gī-zhĭk.
The spirit in the middle of the sky sees me.
[The upper spot denotes the abode of Kī´tshi Man´idō, the "line of vision" extending to the speaker, shown at a corresponding spot below.]

line drawing
Ni-wĭ-we´-wai-a-de´ hi´-me-nai´-o-nā´.
I take my sack and touch him.
The Midē´ will use his sacred Otter-skin sack to touch the candidate.

line drawing
Man´-i-dō wi-kan-ē´, mi-de´-yo.
My medicine is the sacred spirit.
The Midē´ professes to have received the divine gift from Kī´tshi Man´idō; the gifts are seen descending to the hand held up to receive them.

line drawing
Ha-wĭ-ne´ ku-mē´ ni´-kan-nē´?
How do you answer me, my Midē´ friends?

This is addressed to the Midē´ priests (Nika´ni) present, and is an inquiry as to their willingness to proceed. The Midē´wigân is shown, the line running horizontally through it the path of the candidate (or one who has gone through), the two spots within the place of the sacred stone and the post, while the spot to the right of the outside of the inclosure denotes the beginning, or the sweat-lodge, symbolizing the circle of the earth upon the Midē´ chart (Pl. III), those upon the left denoting the three possible degrees of advancement in the future.

Upon the conclusion of the song there is a brief interval, during which all partake of a smoke in perfect silence, making the usual offerings to the four points of the compass, to Kī´tshi Man´idō´, and toward the earth.

The preceptor then says:

Mĭs-sa´i´-a-shi-gwa,	mĭs-sa´-a-shī´-gwa-a	nŏn´-do-nŭng;	ka-kī-nâ

Now is the time, now is the time he hears all of us;

ka-kĭn´-nâ-gi-nŏn´-do-da´g-u-nan´	ga-o´-shī-dōt	mi-dē´-wī-win.

he hears us all the one who made the midē´wiwin.

After this monologue he continues, and addresses to the candidate the midē´ gagī´kwewĭn´, or Midē´ sermon, in the following language, viz:

An-be´-bi-sĭn´-di-wi´-shĭn, wa´-i-ni´-nan;
now listen to me what I am about to say to you;

212

kēsh´-pin-pe´-sin-da´-nin-wĭn	da-ma´-dzhi-shka´	ke´-bi-mâ´-di-si-wĭn´.

If you take heed of that which I say to you shall always continue your life.

U, nun´-gūm,	ke-za´-ki-gi-zi-to mōn	kī´-tshi man´-i-dō	ō´-dik-kĭd´-do-wĭn´;

Now, to-day, I make known to you the great spirit That which he says;

o´-wi-dŏsh kĭd´-di-nĭn´	ki-ī´-kĭd-dō kī´-tshi	man´-i-dō	gi-sa-gi-īg´.

and now this I say to you. This is what says the that he great spirit loves you.

to-wa´-bish-ga´	gi-shtig-wa	a-pī-we-ga-	sa´-gi-sit´-to-wad

It shall be white the sacred object at the time When they shall let it be known

o-sa´-in-di-kĭd´-do-wĭn	ĕ´-kĭd-dōdt kī´-tshi	man´-i-dō

and this is what I say That which he says the great spirit

ŏ´-gi-dĭn´-nĭn	mis-sâ´-wa	ke´-a-ked-de-wó

now this I impart to you even if they say

wa´-ba-ma-tshĭn´ni-bŭdt	mi´-â-ma´ tshī´-ō-nut´	nĭsh-gâd´,

That they saw him dead in this place he shall be Raised again

ini-â-má	a-pe´-ni-nin-dē´	kĭd´-do-wĭn

in this place he puts his trust In my heart in this "saying"

min-nik´ kĭd-da´-	kĭ-o-wĭnk´.	Ka-wī´-ka-da-an´-na-we´-was-si-nan,

the time of the duration Of the world. It shall never fail.

me-ē´-kid-dodt´	man´-i-dō.	Nin´-ne-dzha´-nis

That is what he says, the spirit. My child,

ke-un´-dzhi be-mâ´-dis si´-an.
this shall give you life.

The Midē´ priests then leave the sweat-lodge and stand upon the outside, while the candidate gathers up in his arms a number of small presents, such as tobacco, handkerchiefs, etc., and goes out of the wig´iwam to join the Midē´ priests. The order of marching to the main entrance of the Midē´wigân is then taken up in the following order: First the candidate, next the preceptor, who in turn is followed by the officiating priests, and such others, and members of his family and relatives as desire. At the door of the Midē´wigân all but one of the priests continue forward and take their stations within the inclosure, the preceptor remaining on one side of the candidate, the Midē´ priest upon the other, then all march four times around the outside of the inclosure, toward the left or south, during which time drumming is continued within. Upon the completion of the fourth circuit the candidate is placed so as to face the main entrance of the Midē´wigân. When he is prompted to say:

"Man- un´-ga-bīn´-di-gĕ | o-bŏg´-ga-dī´-nan´, | o-dai´-ye-din´."
Let me come in | and these I put down | my things [gifts].

The presents are then laid upon the ground. The preceptor goes inside, taking with him the gifts deposited by the candidate, and remains standing just within the door and faces the degree post toward the west. Then the chief officiating priest, who has remained at the side of the candidate, turns toward the latter and in a clear, distinct, and exceedingly impressive manner sings the following chant, addressed to Ki′tshi Man′idō whose invisible form is supposed to abide within the Midē′wigan during such ceremonies, stating that the candidate is presented to receive life (the mī′gis) for which he is suffering, and invoking the divine favor.

Hai ya ha man′-i-dō,	hō′, ko-gish′-	ti-bish′-i-gŭng,	hē′, ba-mid′-mi	we-zá-
There is a spirit	ho,	just as the one above,	he,	now sits with me
ni-dzhá-nis, my child	esh-i-gan′-do-we, and now I proclaim,	hē′, hwē′,	mé-a-tshi-bin′-de-gan′-ni-nan, that I enter you here	

213

nōs, man′-i-dō, my good father	dzhi-hō′, ho, spirit,	hwō′, hwo,	sha-wé-nī-mi-shin′, have pity on me,	hē′, hwē he, hwe
a-shig′-wa-bin′-de-gan-nŏk now that I enter him here,	gé-gwa-da-gí-sid he that is suffering		wi-bī-mâ′-di-sīd, for life,	
dé-bwe-daú-wi-shīn believe me	dzhi-bi-mâ′-di-sīd′, that he shall live,		nōs, my father,	
wē′-o-sīm′-in-nan, whose child I am,		hē′, he,	hē′. he.	

The following is the musical notation:
   musical notation
   he-he-he-he yo.

MIDI files: drum , flute , piano (default)

The candidate is then led within the inclosure when all the members of the society arise while he is slowly led around toward the southern side to the extreme end in the west, thence toward the right and back along the western side to the point of beginning. This is done four times. As he starts upon his march, the member nearest the door falls in the line of procession, each member continuing to drop in, at the rear, until the entire assembly is in motion. During this movement there is a monotonous drumming upon the Midē′ drums and the chief officiating priest sings:

| Ni′-sha-bōn′-da shkan | wig′-i-wam | ke-nōn′-dēg, |
| I go through | [the] "house" | the long, i.e., through the Midē′wigân. |

At the fourth circuit, members begin to stop at the places previously occupied by them, the candidate going and remaining with his preceptor to a point just inside the eastern entrance, while the four officiating priests continue around toward the opposite end of the inclosure and station themselves in a semicircle just beyond the degree post, and facing the western door. Upon the ground before them are spread blankets and similar goods, which have been removed from the beams above, and upon which the candidate is to kneel. He is then led to the western extremity of the inclosure where he 214 stands upon the blankets spread upon the ground and faces the four Midē′ priests. The preceptor takes his position behind and a little to one side of the candidate, another assistant being called upon by the preceptor to occupy a corresponding position upon the other side. During this procedure there is gentle drumming which ceases after all have been properly stationed, when the preceptor steps to a point to the side and front of the candidate and nearer the officiating priests, and says:

Mī-i′-shi-gwa′	bŏ′-gi-ta-mo′-nan,	
The time has arrived		that I yield it to you.
mi′-na-nan′-kĕ-ân-dzhi		bi-mâ′-dī-si′-an.
[the midē′migis] that will give you		life.

The preceptor then returns to his position back of and a little to one side of the candidate, when the chief officiating priest sings the following song, accompanying himself upon a small cylindrical midē′drum. The words are: Kit′-ta-no′-do-wē man′-i-do′-wid—you shall hear me, spirit that you are—, and the music is rendered as follows:

musical notation
Kit′ta-no′do-we man′i-dō′wid-hō dō, wē, hē,
Kit′ta-no′do-we man′i-dō-wid-hē, hē, hwē, hē,
Kit′-ta-no′-do-we man′-i-dō′-wic, kit′ta-no′do-wē,
kit′ta-no′do-wid, man′i-do′-wic, man′i-dō′wid-hō, wē, hwē, hē,
Kit′ta-no′dowē′ man′idō′wid, hō, hē, hwē, hē, hē, hwē, hē.

MIDI files: drum , flute , piano (default)

215 After this song is ended the drum is handed to one of the members sitting near by, when the fourth and last of the officiating priests says to the candidate, who is now placed upon his knees:

Mīs-sa′-a-shi′-gwa	ki-bo′-gīs-sē-na-min	tshi′-ma-mâd
Now is the time	that I hope of you	that you shall
bi-mâ′-di-sī-wīn, take life		mī-nē′-sīd. the bead [mi′gis shell.]

This priest then grasps his Midē′ sack as if holding a gun, and, clutching it near the top with the left hand extended, while with the right he clutches it below the middle or near the base, he aims it toward the candidate's left breast and makes a thrust forward toward that target uttering the syllables "yâ, hŏ′, hŏ′, hŏ′, hŏ′, hŏ′, hŏ′," rapidly, rising to a higher key. He recovers his first position and repeats this movement three times, becoming more and more animated, the last time making a vigorous gesture toward the kneeling man's breast as if shooting him. (See Fig. 15, page 192.) While this is going on, the preceptor and his assistants place their hands upon the candidate's shoulders and cause his body to tremble.

Then the next Midē´, the third of the quartette, goes through a similar series of forward movements and thrusts with his Midē´ sack, uttering similar sounds and shooting the sacred mī´gis—life— into the right breast of the candidate, who is agitated still more strongly than before. When the third Midē´, the second in order of precedence, goes through similar gestures and pretends to shoot the mī´gis into the candidate's heart, the preceptors assist him to be violently agitated.

The leading priest now places himself in a threatening attitude and says to the Midē´; "Mī´-dzhi-de´-a-mi-shĭk´"— "put your helping heart with me"—, when he imitates his predecessors by saying, "yâ, hŏ´, hŏ´, hŏ´, hŏ´, hŏ´, hŏ´," at the fourth time aiming the Midē´ sack at the candidate's head, and as the mī´gis is supposed to be shot into it, he falls forward upon the ground, apparently lifeless.

Then the four Midē´ priests, the preceptor and the assistant, lay their Midē´ sacks upon his back and after a few moments a mī´gis shell drops from his mouth—where he had been instructed to retain it. The chief Midē´ picks up the mī´gis and, holding it between the thumb and index finger of the right hand, extending his arm toward the candidate's mouth says "wâ! wâ! hĕ hĕ hĕ hĕ," the last syllable being uttered in a high key and rapidly dropped to a low note; then the same words are uttered while the mī´gis is held toward the east, and in regular succession to the south, to the west, to the north, then toward the sky. During this time the candidate has begun to partially revive and endeavor to get upon his knees, but when the Midē´ finally places the mī´gis into his mouth again, he instantly falls upon the ground, as before. The Midē´ then take up the sacks, each grasping his own as before, and as they pass around the inanimate body they touch it at various points, which causes the 216 candidate to "return to life." The chief priest then says to him, "Ŏ´mishga'n"A —"get up"—which he does; then indicating to the holder of the Midē´ drum to bring that to him, he begins tapping and presently sings the following song:

musical notation

Mi´-si-ni-en´-di-an Mi´si-ni-en´-di-an Mi´-si-ni-en´-dian,

Mi´-si-ni-en´-di-an, Mi´-si-ni-en´-di-an Mi´-si-ni-en´-di-an,

Mi´-si-ni-en´-di-an, Mi´-si-ni-en´-di-an Mi´-si-ni-en´-di-an,

Ni-kan. Hĭū, Hĭū, Hĭu.

MIDI files: drum , flute , piano (default)

The words of the text signify, "This is what I am, my fellow Midē´; I fear all my fellow Midē´." The last syllables, hĭū´, are meaningless.

At the conclusion of the song the preceptor prompts the candidate to ask the chief Midē´:

Ni-kan´	k´kĕ´-manō´-mo´,	ma-dzhi´-an	na´-ka-mō´-in.
Colleague	instruct me,	give me	a song.

In response to which the Midē´ teaches him the following, which is uttered as a monotonous chant, viz:

We´-go-nĕn´	ge-gwed´-dzhi-me-an´,	mi-dē´-wi-wĭn	ke-kwed´-dzhi-me-an´?
What	are you asking,	grand medicine	are you asking?
Ki´-ka-mi´-nin	en-da-wĕn´-da	ma-wi´-nĕn	mi-dē´-wi-wĭn
I will give you	you want me to	give you	"grand medicine"
tshi-da-si-nē´ga´-na-win´-da-mōn;		ki-ĭn´-tshun-di´-nĕ-ma´-so-wĭn,	
always take care of;		you have received it yourself,	
tsho´-a-wa´-nin	di´-sĕ-wan.		
never	forget.		

To this the candidate, who is now a member, replies, ē, yes, i.e., assent, fully agreeing with the statement made by the Midē´, and adds:

Mi-gwĕtsh´	a-shi´-wa-ka-kish´-da-win	be-mâ´-di-si´-an.
Thanks	for giving to me	life.

Then the priests begin to look around in search of spaces in which to seat themselves, saying:
217

Mi´-a-shi´-gwa an´-wâ-bin-da-man	ki´-tshi-	tshi-ō´-we-na´-bi-an.
Now is the time I look around		where we shall be [sit].

and all go to such places as are made, or reserved, for them.

The new member then goes to the pile of blankets, robes, and other gifts and divides them among the four officiating priests, reserving some of less value for the preceptor and his assistant; whereas tobacco is carried around to each person present. All then make an offering of smoke, to the east, south, west, north, toward the center and top of the Midē´wigân—where Ki´tshi Man´idō presides—and to the earth. Then each person blows smoke upon his or her Midē´ sack as an offering to the sacred mī´gis within.

The chief Midē´ advances to the new member and presents him with a new Midē´ sack, made of an otter skin, or possibly of the skin of the mink or weasel, after which he returns to his place. The new member rises, approaches the chief Midē´, who inclines his head to the front, and, while passing both flat hands down over either side,

Mi-gwĕtsh´,	ni-ka´-ni, ni-ka´-ni, ni-ka´-ni, na-ka´.
Thanks	my colleagues, my colleagues, my colleagues.

Then, approaching the next in rank, he repeats the ceremony and continues to do so until he has made the entire circuit of the Midē´wigân.

At the conclusion of this ceremony of rendering thanks to the members of the society for their presence, the newly elected Midē´ returns to his place and, after placing within his Midē´ sack his mī´gis, starts out anew to test his own powers. He approaches the person seated nearest the eastern entrance, on the south side, and, grasping his sack in a manner similar to that of the officiating priests, makes threatening motions toward the Midē´ as if to shoot him, saying, "yâ, hŏ´, hŏ´, hŏ´, hŏ´, hŏ´," gradually raising his voice to a higher key. At the fourth movement he makes a quick thrust toward his victim, whereupon the latter falls forward upon the ground. He then proceeds to the next, who is menaced in a similar manner and who likewise becomes apparently unconscious from the powerful effects of the mī´gis. This is continued until all persons present have been subjected to the influence of the mī´gis in the possession of the new member. At the third or fourth experiment the first subject revives and sits up, the others recovering in regular order a short time after having been "shot at," as this procedure is termed.

When all of the Midē´ have recovered a very curious ceremony takes place. Each one places his mī´gis shell upon the right palm and, grasping the Midē´ sack with the left hand, moves around the inclosure and exhibits his mī´gis to everyone present, constantly uttering the word "hŏ´, hŏ´, hŏ´, hŏ´," in a quick, low tone. During this period there is a mingling of all the persons present, each endeavoring to attract the attention of the others. Each Midē´ then pretends to swallow his mī´gis, when suddenly there are sounds of violent coughing, as if the actors were strangling, and soon thereafter they gag and spit out upon the ground the mī´gis, upon which each one falls apparently dead. In a few moments, however, they recover, take up the little shells again and pretend to swallow them. As the Midē´ return to their respective places the mī´gis is restored to its receptacle in the Midē´ sack.

Food is then brought into the Midē´wigân and all partake of it at the expense of the new member.

After the feast, the older Midē´ of high order, and possibly the officiating priests, recount the tradition of the Ani´shinâ´bēg and the origin of the Midē´wiwin, together with speeches relating to the benefits to be derived through a knowledge thereof, and sometimes, tales of individual success and exploits. When the inspired ones have given utterance to their thoughts and feelings, their memories and their boastings, and the time of adjournment has almost arrived, the new member gives an evidence of his skill as a singer and a Midē´. Having acted upon the suggestion of his preceptor, he has prepared some songs and learned them, and now for the first time the opportunity presents itself for him to gain admirers and influential friends, a sufficient number of whom he will require to speak well of him, and to counteract the evil which will be spoken of him by enemies—for enemies are numerous and may be found chiefly among those who are not fitted for the society of the Midē´, or who have failed to attain the desired distinction.

The new member, in the absence of a Midē´ drum of his own, borrows one from a fellow Midē´ and begins to beat it gently, increasing the strokes in intensity as he feels more and more inspired, then sings a song (Pl. X, D), of which the following are the words, each line being repeated ad libitum, viz:

mnemonic song
Plate X.d. Mnemonic Song.
line drawing Wi/in gn-wi´-wik ka´-ni-an.
    The spirit has made sacred the place in which I live.
    The singer is shown partly within, and partly above his wigwam, the latter being represented by the lines upon either side, and crossing his body.
line drawing Kaw-i-yan´ pi-ma´-ti-su´-i-ŭn en´-da-yan´.
    The spirit gave the "medicine" which we receive.
    The upper inverted crescent is the arch of the sky, the magic influence descending, like rain upon the earth, the latter being shown by the horizontal line at the bottom.
vertical lines Rest.

219 Nin´-nik-ka´-ni man´-i-dō.
    I too have taken the medicine he gave us.
drawing The speaker's arm, covered with mī´gis, or magic influence, reaches toward the sky to receive from Ki´tshi Man´idō the divine favor of a Midē's power.
line drawing Kaw-kŏg´-ō-ĭ-yan´.
    I brought life to the people.
    The Thunderer, the one who causes the rains, and consequently life to vegetation, by which the Indian may sustain life.
line drawing Be-wing´-se ma-kō-yan.
    I have come to the medicine lodge also.
    The Bear Spirit, one of the guardians of the Midē´wiwin, was also present, and did not oppose the singer's entrance.
line drawing Kaw-i-ka-mi´-ni-ni´-ta.
    We spirits are talking together.
    The singer compares himself and his colleagues to spirits, i.e., those possessing supernatural powers, and communes with them as an equal.
line drawing On-wi-i-gi-shĭnk-ni´-yo.
    The mī´gis is on my body.
    The magic power has been put into his body by the Midē priests.
line drawing Ni-wi-naw´-i-dō ni´-yăn.
    The spirit has put away all my sickness.
    He has received new life, and is, henceforth, free from the disturbing influences of evil man´idōs.

As the sun approaches the western horizon, the Midē´ priests emerge from the western door of the Midē´wigân and go to their respective wig´iwams, where they partake of their regular evening repast, after which the remainder of the evening is spent in paying calls upon other members of the society, smoking, etc.

The preceptor and his assistant return to the Midē´wigân at nightfall, remove the degree post and plant it at the head of the wig´iwam—that part directly opposite the entrance—occupied by the new member. Two stones are placed at the base of the post, to represent the two forefeet of the bear Man´idō through whom life was also given to the Ani´shinâ´bēg.

If there should be more than one candidate to receive a degree the entire number, if not too great, is taken into the Midē´wigân for initiation at the same time; and if one day suffices to transact the 220 business for which the meeting was called the Indians return to their respective homes upon the following morning. If, however, arrangements have been made to advance a member to a higher degree, the necessary changes and appropriate arrangement of the interior of the Midē´wigân are begun immediately after the society has adjourned.

DESCRIPTIVE NOTES.

The mī´gis referred to in this description of the initiation consists of a small white shell, of almost any species, but the one believed to resemble the form of the mythical mī´gis is similar to the cowrie, Cypræa moneta, L., and is figured at No. 1 on Pl. XI . Nearly all of the shells employed for this purpose are foreign species, and have no doubt been obtained from the traders. The shells found in the country of the Ojibwa are of rather delicate structure, and it is probable that the salt water shells are employed as a substitute chiefly because of their less frangible character. The mī´gis of the other degrees are presented on the same plate, but special reference to them will be made. No. 2 represents the mī´gis in the possession of the chief Midē priest of the society at Leech Lake, Minnesota, and consists of a pearl-white Helix (sp?).

plate described in text
  Plate XI. Sacred Objects.
  The Midē´ sack represented in No. 7 (Pl. XI .) is made of the skin of a mink—Putorius vison, Gapp. White, downy feathers are secured to the nose, as an additional ornament. In this sack are carried the sacred objects belonging to its owner, such as colors for facial ornamentation, and the magic red powder employed in the preparation of hunters´ songs; effigies and other contrivances to prove to the incredulous the genuineness of the Midē´ pretensions, sacred songs, amulets, and other small man´idōs—abnormal productions to which they attach supernatural properties—invitation sticks, etc.

hawk's leg as described in t
Fig. 19. —Hawk-leg fetish.
221 In Fig. 19 is reproduced a curious abnormal growth which was in the possession of a Midē´ near Red Lake, Minnesota. It consists of the leg of a Goshawk—Astur atricapillus, Wilson—from the outer inferior condyle of the right tibia of which had projected a supernumerary leg that terminated in two toes, the whole abnormality being about one-half the size and length of the natural leg and toes.

This fetish was highly prized by its former owner, and was believed to be a medium whereby the favor of the Great Thunderer, or Thunder God, might be invoked and his anger appeased. This deity is represented in pictography by the eagle, or frequently by one of the Falconidæ; hence it is but natural that the superstitious should look with awe and reverence upon such an abnormality on one of the terrestrial representatives of this deity.

A Midē´ of the first degree, who may not be enabled to advance further in the mysteries of the Midē´wiwin, owing to his inability to procure the necessary quantity of presents and gifts which he is required to pay to new preceptors and to the officiating priests—the latter demanding goods of double the value of those given as an entrance to the first degree—may, however, accomplish the acquisition of additional knowledge by purchasing it from individual Midē´. It is customary with Midē´ priests to exact payment for every individual remedy or secret that may be imparted to another who may desire such information. This practice is not entirely based upon mercenary motives, but it is firmly believed that when a secret or remedy has been paid, for it can not be imparted for nothing, as then its virtue would be impaired, if not entirely destroyed, by the man´idō or guardian spirit under whose special protection it may be supposed to be held or controlled.

Under such circumstances certain first degree Midē´ may become possessed of alleged magic powers which are in reality part of the accomplishments of the Midē´ of the higher degrees; but, for the mutual protection of the members of the society, they generally hesitate to impart anything that may be considered of high value. The usual kind of knowledge sought consists of the magic properties and use of plants, to the chief varieties of which reference will be made in connection with the next degree.

There is one subject, however, which first-degree Midē´ seek enlightment upon, and that is the preparation of the "hunter's medicine" and the pictographic drawings employed in connection therewith. The compound is made of several plants, the leaves and roots of which are ground into powder. A little of this is put into the gun barrel, with the bullet, and sometimes a small pinch is dropped upon the track of the animal to compel it to halt at whatever place it may be when the powder is so sprinkled upon the ground.

The method generally employed to give to the hunter success is as follows: When anyone contemplates making a hunting trip, he first visits the Midē´, giving him a present of tobacco before announcing 222 the object of his visit and afterwards promising to give him such and such portions of the animal which he may procure. The Midē´, if satisfied with the gift, produces his pipe and after making an offering to Ki´tshi Man´idō for aid in the preparation of his "medicine," and to appease the anger of the man´idō who controls the class of animals desired, sings a song, one of his own composition, after which he will draw with a sharp-pointed bone or nail, upon a small piece of birch bark, the outline of the animal desired by the applicant. The place of the heart of the animal is indicated by a puncture upon which a small quantity of vermilion is carefully rubbed, this color being very efficacious toward effecting the capture of the animal and the punctured heart insuring its death.

figure described in text
Fig. 20. —Hunter's medicine.

Frequently the heart is indicated by a round or triangular figure, from which a line extends toward the mouth, generally designated the life line, i.e., that magic power may reach its heart and influence the life of the subject designated. Fig. 20 is a reproduction of the character drawn upon a small oval piece of birch bark, which had been made by a Midē´ to insure the death of two bears. Another example is presented in Fig. 21, a variety of animals being figured and a small quantity of vermilion being rubbed upon the heart of each. In some instances the representation of animal forms is drawn by the Midē´ not upon birch bark, but directly upon sandy earth or a bed of ashes, either of which affords a smooth surface. For this purpose he uses a sharply pointed piece of wood, thrusts it into the region of the heart, and afterwards sprinkles upon this a small quantity of powder consisting of magic plants and vermilion. These performances are not conducted in public, but after the regular mystic ceremony has been conducted by the Midē´ the information is delivered with certain injunctions as to the course of procedure, direction, 223 etc. In the latter method of drawing the outline upon the sand or upon ashes, the result is made known with such directions as may be deemed necessary to insure success.

figure described in text
Fig. 21. —Hunter's medicine.

For the purpose of gaining instruction and success in the disposition of his alleged medicines, the Midē´ familiarizes himself with the topography and characteristics of the country extending over a wide area, to ascertain the best feeding grounds of the various animals and their haunts at various seasons. He keeps himself informed by also skillfully conducting inquiries of returning hunters, and thus becomes possessed of a large amount of valuable information respecting the natural history of the surrounding country, by which means he can, with a tolerable amount of certainty, direct a hunter to the best localities for such varieties of game as may be particularly desired by him.

drum head ass described in
Fig. 22. —Wâbĕnō´ drum.

In his incantations a Wâbĕnō´ uses a drum resembling a tambourine. A hoop made of ash wood is covered with a piece of rawhide, tightly stretched while wet. Upon the upper surface is painted a mythic figure, usually that of his tutelaly daimon. An example of this kind is from Red Lake, Minnesota, presented in Fig. 22. The human figure is painted red, while the outline of the head is black, as are also the waving lines extending from the head. These lines denote superior power. When drumming upon this figure, the Wâbĕnō´ chants and is thus more easily enabled to invoke the assistance of his man´idō.

Women, as before remarked, may take the degrees of the Midē´wiwin, but, so far as could be ascertained, their professions pertain chiefly to the treatment of women and children and to tattooing for the cure of headache and chronic neuralgia.

Tattooing is accomplished by the use of finely powdered charcoal, soot or gunpowder, the pricking instrument being made by tying together a small number of needles; though formerly, it is said, fish spines or sharp splinters of bone were used for the purpose. The marks consist of round spots of one-half to three-fourths of an inch in diameter immediately over the afflicted part, the intention being to drive out the demon. Such spots are usually found upon the temples, though an occasional one may be found on the forehead or over the nasal eminence.

When the pain extends over considerable space the tattoo marks are smaller, and are arranged in rows or continuous lines. Such marks may be found upon some individuals to run outward over either or both cheeks from the alæ of the nose to a point near the 224 lobe of the ear, clearly indicating that the tattooing was done for toothache or neuralgia.

The female Midē´ is usually present at the initiation of new members, but her duties are mainly to assist in the singing and to make herself generally useful in connection with the preparation of the medicine feast.

SECOND DEGREE.

The inclosure within which the second degree of the Midē´wiwin is conferred, resembles in almost every respect that of the first, the only important difference being that there are two degree posts instead of one. A diagram is presented in Fig. 23. The first post is planted a short distance beyond the middle of the floor—toward the western door—and is similar to the post of the first degree, i.e., red, with a band of green around the top, upon which is perched the stuffed body of an owl; the kŏ-kŏ´-kŏ-ō´. The second post, of similar size, is painted red, and over the entire surface of it are spots of white made by applying clay with the finger tips. (Pl. XV, No. 2.) These spots are symbolical of the sacred mī´gis, the great number of them denoting increased power of the magic influence which fills the Midē´wigân. A small cedar tree is also planted at each of the outer angles of the inclosure.

midewigan as described in text
Fig. 23. —Diagram of Midē´wigân of the second degree.

The sweat-lodge, as before, is erected at some distance east of the main entrance of the Midē´wigân, but a larger structure is arranged upon a similar plan; more ample accommodations must be provided to permit a larger gathering of Midē´ priests during the period of preparation and instruction of the candidate.

PREPARATION OF CANDIDATE.

A Midē´ of the first degree is aware of the course to be pursued by him when he contemplates advancement into the next higher grade. Before making known to the other members his determination, he is compelled to procure, either by purchase or otherwise, such a quantity of blankets, robes, peltries, and other articles of apparel or ornament as will amount in value to twice the sum at which were estimated the gifts presented at his first initiation. A year or more usually elapses before this can be accomplished, as but one hunting season intervenes before the next annual meeting of the society, when furs are in their prime; and fruits and maple sugar can be gathered but once during the season, and these may be converted into money with which to purchase presents not always found 225 at the Indian traders' stores. Friends may be called upon to advance goods to effect the accomplishment of his desire, but such loans must be returned in kind later on, unless otherwise agreed. When a candidate feels convinced that he has gathered sufficient material to pay for his advancement, he announces to those members of the society who are of a higher grade than the first degree that he wishes to present himself at the proper time for initiation. This communication is made to eight of the highest or officiating priests, in his own wig'iwam, to which they have been specially invited. A feast is prepared and partaken of, after which he presents to each some tobacco, and smoking is indulged in for the purpose of making proper offerings, as already described. The candidate then informs his auditors of his desire and enumerates the various goods and presents which he has procured to offer at the proper time. The Midē' priests sit in silence and meditate; but as they have already been informally aware of the applicant's wish, they are prepared as to the answer they will give, and are governed according to the estimated value of the gifts. Should the decision of the Midē' priests be favorable, the candidate procures the services of one of those present to assume the office of instructor or preceptor, to whom, as well as to the officiating priests, he displays his ability in his adopted specialties in medical magic, etc. He seeks, furthermore, to acquire additional information upon the preparation of certain secret remedies, and to this end he selects a preceptor who has the reputation of possessing it.

For acting in the capacity of instructor, a Midē' priest receives blankets, horses, and whatever may be mutually agreed upon between himself and his pupil. The meetings take place at the instructor's wig'iwam at intervals of a week or two; and sometimes during the autumn months, preceding the summer in which the initiation is to be conferred, the candidate is compelled to resort to a sudatory and take a vapor bath, as a means of purgation preparatory to his serious consideration of the sacred rites and teachings with which his mind "and heart" must henceforth be occupied, to the exclusion of everything that might tend to divert his thoughts.

What the special peculiarities and ceremonials of initiation into the second degree may have been in former times, it is impossible to ascertain at this late day. The only special claims for benefits to be derived through this advancement, as well as into the third and fourth degrees, are, that a Midē' upon his admission into a new degree receives the protection of that Man'idō alleged and believed to be the special guardian of such degree, and that the repetition of initiation adds to the magic powers previously received by the initiate. In the first degree the sacred mīgis was "shot" into the two sides, the heart, and head of the candidate, whereas in the second degree this sacred, or magic, influence is directed by the priests 226 toward the candidate's joints, in accordance with a belief entertained by some priests and referred to in connection with the Red Lake chart presented on Pl. III. The second, third, and fourth degrees are practically mere repetitions of the first, and the slight differences between them are noted under their respective captions.

In addition to a recapitulation of the secrets pertaining to the therapeutics of the Midē', a few additional magic remedies are taught the candidate in his preparatory instruction. The chief of these are described below.

Ma-kwa' wī'-i-sŏp, "Bear's Gall," and Pi'-zhi-ki wī'-i-sŏp, "Ox Gall," are both taken from the freshly killed animal and hung up to dry. It is powdered as required, and a small pinch of it is dissolved in water, a few drops of which are dropped into the ear of a patient suffering from earache.

Gō'-gi-mish (gen. et sp.?).—A plant, described by the preceptor as being about 2 feet in height, having black bark and clusters of small red flowers.

1. The bark is scraped from the stalk, crushed and dried. When it is to be used the powder is put into a small bag of cloth and soaked in hot water to extract the virtue. It is used to expel evil man'idōs which cause obstinate coughs, and is also administered to consumptives. The quantity of bark derived from eight stems, each 10 inches long, makes a large dose. When a Midē' gives this medicine to a patient, he fills his pipe and smokes, and before the tobacco is all consumed the patient vomits.

2. The root of this plant mixed with the following is used to produce paralysis of the mouth. In consequence of the power it possesses it is believed to be under the special protection of the Midē' Man'idō, i.e., Ki'tshi Man'idō.

The compound is employed also to counteract the evil intentions, conjurations, or other charms of so-called bad Midē', Wâbĕnō', and Jĕs'sakkīd'.

Tzhi-bē'-gŏp—"Ghost Leaf."

After the cuticle is removed from the roots the thick under-bark is crushed into a powder. It is mixed with Gō'gimish.

Dzhi-bai'-ĕ-mŏk'-ke-zĭn'—"Ghost Moccasin;" "Puff-ball."

The spore-dust of the ball is carefully reserved to add to the above mixture.

O-kwē'-mish—"Bitter Black Cherry."

The inner bark of branches dried and crushed is also added.

Nē'-wĕ—"Rattlesnake" (*Crotalus durissus, L.*).

The reptile is crushed and the blood collected, dried, and used in a pulverulent form. After partially crushing the body it is hung up and the drippings collected and dried. Other snakes may be employed as a substitute.

It is impossible to state the nature of the plants mentioned in the above compound, as they are not indigenous to the vicinity of White Earth, Minnesota, but are procured from Indians living in the eastern extremity of the State and in Wisconsin. Poisonous plants are of rare occurrence in this latitude, and if any actual poisonous properties exist in the mixture they may be introduced by the Indian himself, as strychnia is frequently to be purchased at almost any of the stores, to be used in the extermination of noxious animals. Admitting that crotalus venom may be present, the introduction into the human circulation of this substance would without doubt produce death and not paralysis of the facial muscles, and if taken into the stomach it quickly undergoes chemical change when brought in contact with the gastric juice, as is well known from experiments made by several well known physiologists, and particularly by Dr. Coxe (Dispensatory, 1839), who employed the contents of the venom sack, mixed with bread, for the cure of rheumatism.

I mention this because of my personal knowledge of six cases at White Earth, in which paralysis of one side of the face occurred soon after the Midē´ administered this compound. In nearly all of them the distortion disappeared after a lapse of from six weeks to three months, though one is known to have continued for several years with no signs of recovery. The Catholic missionary at White Earth, with whom conversation was held upon this subject, feels impressed that some of the so-called "bad Midē´" have a knowledge of some substance, possibly procured from the whites, which they attempt to employ in the destruction of enemies, rivals, or others. It may be possible that the instances above referred to were cases in which the dose was not sufficient to kill the victim, but was enough to disable him temporarily. Strychnia is the only substance attainable by them that could produce such symptoms, and then only when given in an exceedingly small dose. It is also alleged by almost every one acquainted with the Ojibwa that they do possess poisons, and that they employ them when occasion demands in the removal of personal enemies or the enemies of those who amply reward the Midē´ for such service.

invitation sticks
Plate XII. Invitation Sticks.

When the time of ceremony of initiation approaches, the chief Midē´ priest sends out a courier to deliver to each member an invitation to attend (Pl. XII), while the candidate removes his wig´iwam to the vicinity of the place where the Midē´wigân has been erected. On the fifth day before the celebration he visits the sweat-lodge, where he takes his first vapor bath, followed on the next by another; on the following day he takes the third bath, after which his preceptor visits him. After making an offering to Ki´tshi Man´idō the priest sings a song, of which the characters are reproduced in Pl. XIII , A . The Ojibwa words employed in singing are given in the first lines, and are said to be the ancient phraseology as taught for many generations. They are archaic, to a great extent, and have additional meaningless syllables inserted, and used as suffixes which are intoned to prolong notes. The second line of the Ojibwa text consists of the words as they are spoken at the present time, to each of which is added the interpretation. The radical similarity between the two is readily perceived.

mnemonic song
Plate XIII.a. Mnemonic Song.
line Hi´-na-wi´-a-ni-ka. (As sung.)
draw-ing We´-me-a´ ni-kan mi´-sha man´-i-dō

I am crying my colleague great spirit.

ni-wa´-ma-bi-go´ ma´-wĭ-yan´.

He sees me crying.

[The singer is represented as in close relationship or communion with Ki´tshi Man´idō, the circle denoting union; the short zigzag lines within which, in this instance, represent the tears, i.e., "eye rain," directed toward the sky.]

Ki-nŭn´-no, hē´, ki-mun´-i-dō´-we, hē´,
line esh´-i-ha´-ni. (As sung.)
draw-ing Gi- ni-kan´ ē-zhi-an. nŭn´-dōn

I hear you, colleague, what you say to me.

[The singer addresses the Otter Spirit, whose figure is emerging from the Midē´wigân of which he is the chief guardian.]

line Tē´-ti-wâ´-tshi-wi-mō´ a-ni´-me-ga´-si. (As sung.)
draw-ing Tē´-ti-wâ´-tshŏ- ni-mī´-gĭ-tâg´ sĭm.

He will tell you (—inform you) [of] my migis.

tē´-ti-wa´-tshĭ-mo-ta´ âg.

He it is who will tell you.

[The reference is to a superior spirit as indicated by the presence of horns, and the zigzag line upon the breast. The words signify that Ki´tshi Man´idō will make known to the candidate the presence within his body of the mī´gis, when the proper time arrives.]

vertical lines — Rest, or pause, in the song.

During this interval another smoke offering is made, in which the Midē´ priest is joined by the candidate.

line Hĭu´-a-me´-da-ma´ ki´-a-wēn´-da-mag man´-i-dō´-wĭt hĭu´-a-wen´-da-mag. (As sung.)
draw-ing Ki-wĭn´-da-mag´-ū-nan man´-i-dō´-wid.

He tells us he is [one] of the man´idōs.

[This ma´nidō is the same as that referred to in the above-named phrase. This form is different, the four spots denoting the four sacred mī´gis points upon his body, the short radiating lines referring to the abundance of magic powers with which it is filled.]

line Wa´-sa-wa-dī´, hē´, wen´-da-na-draw-ma´, mĭ-tē´-wi. (As sung.)
ing Wa´-sa-wa´-dŭn´-da-na-ma´

I get it from afar
mi-dē´-wi-wĭn´.
The "grand medicine."
[The character represents a leg, with a magic line drawn across the middle, to signify that the distance is accomplished only through the medium of supernatural powers. The place "from afar" refers to the abode of Ki´tshi Man´idō.]

line drawing Ki-go´-na-bi-hi ē´-ni-na mi-tē´. (As sung.)
Ki-do´-na-bī-in´ mi-dē´-wi-wĭn-ni-ni´
I place you there "in the grand medicine" (among the "Midē´ people")
a-bit´-da-win´.
Half way (in the Midē´wigân).
[The Midē´ priest informs the candidate that the second initiation will advance the candidate half way into the secrets of the Midē´wigân. The candidate is then placed so that his body will have more magic influence and power as indicated by the zigzag lines radiating from it toward the sky.]

229 Hi´-sha-we-ne´-me-go´, hē´, nē´.
Ni-go´-tshi-mi, hē´. (As sung.)

line drawing Nĭ´-sha-we´-ni-mi-go´ ĕ´-ne-mâ´-bi-dzhĭk.
They have pity on me those who are sitting here.
[This request is made to the invisible man´idōs who congregate in the Midē´wigân during the ceremonies, and the statement implies that they approve of the candidate's advancement.]

Another smoke offering is made upon the completion of this song, after which both individuals retire to their respective habitations. Upon the following day, that being the one immediately preceding the day of ceremony, the candidate again repairs to the sudatory to take a last vapor bath, after the completion of which he awaits the coming of his preceptor for final conversation and communion with man´idōs respecting the step he is prepared to take upon the morrow.

The preceptor's visit is merely for the purpose of singing to the candidate, and impressing him with the importance of the rites of the Midē´wigân. After making the usual offering of tobacco smoke the preceptor becomes inspired and sings a song, the following being a reproduction of the one employed by him at this stage of the preparatory instruction. (See Pl. XIII, B.)

mnemonic song
Plate XIII.b. Mnemonic Song.

line drawing Man´-i-dō´, man´-i-dō´, hē´, nē, hē´, nē´.
Spirit, spirit,
Ni´-man- win´-da-bi-an´.
i-dō´
I am a (is) the reason why I
spirit am here.
[The zigzag lines extending downward and outward from the mouth indicate singing. He has reached the power of a man´idō, and is therefore empowered to sit within the sacred inclosure of the Midē´wigân, to which he alludes.]

line drawing Dā´-bī-wā-ni´, ha´, hē´, A´-nĭn, e-kō´-wē-an´.
Drifting snow, why do I sing.
[The first line is sung, but no interpretation of the words could be obtained, and it was alleged that the second line contained the idea to be expressed. The horizontal curve denotes the sky, the vertical zigzag lines indicating falling snow—though being exactly like the lines employed to denote rain. The drifting snow is likened to a shower of delicate mī´gis shells or spots, and inquiry is made of it to account for the feeling of inspiration experienced by the singer, as this shower of mī´gis descends from the abode of Ki´tshi Man´idō and is therefore, in this instance, looked upon as sacred.]

vertical lines Rest, or pause.

230 Gi-man´-i-dō´-wē, ni´-me-ne´-ki-nan´ wan-da.
line drawing Gi´-a-wĭngk, gi-man´-i-dō´-a-ni-min´,
Your body, I believe it is a spirit.
Gi-a-wĭngk.
your body.
[The first line is sung, but the last word could not be satisfactorily explained. The first word, as now pronounced, is Ki´tshi Man´idō, and the song is addressed to him. The curved line, from which the arm protrudes, is the Midē´wigân and the arm itself is that of the speaker in the attitude of adoration: reaching upward in worship and supplication.]

line drawing Pi-nē´-si ne´-pi- ni´-ge-gē´-nĭ´-a kwe-a
The bird as I the falcon promise
mi-we´-tshi-man´-i-dō´-wid.
the reason he is a spirit.
[The second word is of archaic form and no agreement concerning its correct signification could be reached by the Midē´. The meaning of the phrase appears to be that Ki´tshi Man´idō promised to create the Thunderbird, one of the man´idōs. The falcon is here taken as a representative of that deity, the entire group of Thunderers being termed a-ni´-mi-ki´.]

line drawing Zhĭn´-gwe mi´-shi-ma-kwa´
Makes a great noise the bear.
we´-dzhi-wa-ba-mok- kŭn-kwēd´ nēt´.
the reason I am of flame.
[The character of the bear represents the great bear spirit of the malevolent type, a band about his body indicating his spirit form. By means of his power and influence the singer has become endowed with the ability of changing his form into that of the bear, and in this guise accomplishing good or evil. The reference to flame (fire) denotes

line drawing	Ní'-a-wen'-din-da-sa', ha', sa', man'-i-dō'-wid.	
	Gí'-a-wĭngk ĭn'-do-sa	man'-i-dō'-wid.
	In your body I put it	the spirit.

[The first line is sung, and is not of the modern style of spoken language. The second line signifies that the arm of Kĭ'tshi Man'idō, through the intermediary of the Midē' priest, will put the spirit, i.e., the mī'gis, into the body of the candidate.]

The singer accompanies his song either by using a short baton of wood, termed "singing stick" or the Midē' drum. After the song is completed another present of tobacco is given to the preceptor, and after making an offering of smoke both persons return to their respective wig'iwams. Later in the evening the preceptor calls upon the candidate, when both, with the assistance of friends, carry the presents to the Midē'wigân, where they are suspended from the rafters, 231 to be ready for distribution after the initiation on the following day. Several friends of the candidate, who are Midē', are stationed at the doors of the Midē'wigân to guard against the intrusion of the uninitiated, or the possible abstraction of the gifts by strangers.

INITIATION OF CANDIDATE.

The candidate proceeds early on the morning of the day of initiation to take possession of the sweat-lodge, where he awaits the coming of his preceptor and the eight officiating priests. He has an abundance of tobacco with which to supply all the active participants, so that they may appease any feeling of opposition of the man'idōs toward the admission of a new candidate, and to make offerings of tobacco to the guardian spirit of the second degree of the Midē'wiwin. After the usual ceremony of smoking individual songs are indulged in by the Midē' priests until such time as they may deem it necessary to proceed to the Midē'wigân, where the members of the society have long since gathered and around which is scattered the usual crowd of spectators. The candidate leads the procession from the sweat-lodge to the eastern entrance of the Midē'wigân, carrying an ample supply of tobacco and followed by the priests who chant. When the head of the procession arrives at the door of the sacred inclosure a halt is made, the priests going forward and entering. The drummer, stationed within, begins to drum and sing, while the preceptor and chief officiating priest continue their line of march around the inclosure, going by way of the south or left hand. Eight circuits are made, the last terminating at the main or eastern entrance. The drumming then ceases and the candidate is taken to the inner side of the door, when all the members rise and stand in their places. The officiating priests approach and stand near the middle of the inclosure, facing the candidate, when one of them says to the Midē' priest beside the latter: O-da'-pĭn a-sē'-ma—"Take it, the tobacco," whereupon the Midē' spoken to relieves the candidate of the tobacco and carries it to the middle of the inclosure, where it is laid upon a blanket spread upon the ground. The preceptor then takes from the cross-poles some of the blankets or robes and gives them to the candidate to hold. One of the malevolent spirits which oppose the entrance of a stranger is still supposed to remain with the Midē'wigân, its body being that of a serpent, like flames of fire, reaching from the earth to the sky. He is called I'-shi-ga-nē'-bĭ-gŏg—"Big-Snake." To appease his anger the candidate must make a present; so the preceptor says for the candidate:

Ka-wī'-nĭ-na-ga'	wa'-ba-ma'-si-ba'-shĭ-gĭ'-ne-gēt'?
Do you not see	how he carries the goods?

This being assented to by the Midē' priests the preceptor takes the blankets and deposits them near the tobacco upon the ground. Slight taps upon the Midē' drum are heard and the candidate is led 232 toward the left on his march round the interior of the Midē'wigân, the officiating priests following and being followed in succession by all others present. The march continues until the eighth passage round, when the members begin to step back into their respective places, while the officiating Midē' finally station themselves with their backs toward the westernmost degree post, and face the door at the end of the structure. The candidate continues round to the western end, faces the Midē' priests, and all sit down. The following song is then sung, which may be the individual production of the candidate (Pl. XIII, C). A song is part of the ritual, though it is not necessary that the candidate should sing it, as the preceptor may do so for him. In the instance under my observation the song was an old one (which had been taught the candidate), as the archaic form of pronunciation indicates. Each of the lines is repeated as often as the singer may desire, the prolongation of the song being governed by his inspired condition. The same peculiarity governs the insertion, between words and at the end of lines, of apparently meaningless vowel sounds, to reproduce and prolong the last notes sounded. This may be done ad libitum, rythmical accentuation being maintained by gently tapping upon the Midē' drum.

mnemonic song

Plate XIII.c. Mnemonic Song.

line drawing	Hīn'-de hĕn'-da man'-i-dō, hō', ni'-sha-bon'-de man'-i-dō'-en-dât.

Where is the spirit lodge? I go through it.

[The oblong structure represents the Midē'wigân, the arm upon the left indicating the course of the path leading through it, the latter being shown by a zigzag line.]

line drawing	Nin-gō'-sa mĭ-dē'-kwe ni-ka' crawna'-ska-wa'.

I am afraid of the "grand medicine" woman; I go to her.

A leg is shown to signify locomotion. The singer fears the opposition of a Midē′ priestess and will conciliate her.

line drawing Kawi-sa′ hi′-a-tshi′-mĭn-dē′ man′-ski-kī′, dē′, hē′, hē′.

Kinsmen who speak of me, they see the striped sky.

A person of superior power, as designated by the horns attached to the head. The lines from the mouth signify voice or speech, while the horizontal lines denote the stratus clouds, the height above the earth of which illustrates the direction of the abode of the spirit whose conversation, referring to the singer, is observed crossing them as short vertical zigzag lines; i.e., voice lines.

line drawing Ke′-na-nan′-do-mē′ ko-nō′-ne-nĕk ka-ne-hē′ nin-ko′-tshi nan′-no-me′.

The cloud looks to me for medicine.

[The speaker has become so endowed with the power of magic influence that he has preference with the superior Man′idōs. The magic influence is shown descending to the hand which reaches beyond the cloud indicated by the oblong square upon the forearm.]

233 Rest, after which dancing begins.

vertical lines

line drawing Wa-tshu′-a-nē′ ke′-ba-bing′-e-ing′, wa-dzhū.

Going into the mountains.

The singer's thoughts go to the summit to commune with Ki′tshi Man′idō. He is shown upon the summit.

line drawing Hi′-mĕ-dē′-wa hen′-dĕ-a he′-na.

The grand medicine affects me.

In his condition he appeals to Ki′tshi Man′idō for aid. The arms represent the act of supplication.

line drawing Hai′-an-go ho′-ya o′-gĕ-ma, ha′.

The chief goes out.

The arms grasp a bear—the Bear Man′idō—and the singer intimates that he desires the aid of that powerful spirit, who is one of the guardians of the Midē′wigân.

line drawing Nish-wē′ ni-mē′-hi-gō′, hē′, ni-gō′-tshi-mi′-go-we, hē′.

Have pity on me wherever I have medicine.

The speaker is filled with magic influence, upon the strength of which he asks the Bear to pity and to aid him.

line drawing Wi′-so-mi′-ko-wē′ hĕ-a-za-wē′-ne-ne-gō′, hō′.

I am the beaver; have pity on me.

This is said to indicate that the original maker of the mnemonic song was of the Beaver totem or gens.

line drawing Haw′-ta-no-wik′-ko-we′ de-wĕn′-da ĕn-da-â′-dân.

I wish to know what is the matter with me.

The singer feels peculiarly impressed by his surroundings in the Midē′wigân, because the sacred man′idōs have filled his body with magic powers. These are shown by the zigzag or waving lines descending to the earth.

As each of the preceding lines or verses is sung in such a protracted manner as to appear like a distinct song, the dancers, during the intervals of rest, always retire to their places and sit down. 234 The dancing is not so energetic as many of those commonly indulged in for amusement only. The steps consist of two treading movements made by each foot in succession. Keeping time with the drum-beats, at the same time there is a shuffling movement made by the dancer forward, around and among his companions, but getting back toward his place before the verse is ended. The attitude during these movements consists in bending the body forward, while the knees are bent, giving one the appearance of searching for a lost object. Those who do not sing give utterance to short, deep grunts, in accordance with the alternate heavier strokes upon the drum.

As the dancing ceases, and all are in their proper seats, the preceptor, acting for the candidate, approaches the pile of tobacco and distributes a small quantity to each one present, when smoking is indulged in, preceded by the usual offering to the east, the south, the west, the north, the sky and the earth.

After the completion of this ceremonial an attendant carries the Midē′ drum to the southeast angle of the inclosure, where it is delivered to the drummer; then the officiating priests rise and approach within two or three paces of the candidate as he gets upon his knees. The preceptor and the assistant who is called upon by him take their places immediately behind and to either side of the candidate, and the Midē′ priest lowest in order of precedence begins to utter quick, deep tones, resembling the sound hŏ′, hŏ′, hŏ′, hŏ′, hŏ′, at the same time grasping his midē′ sack with both hands, as if it were a gun, and moving it in a serpentine and interrupted manner toward one of the large joints of the candidate's arms or legs. At the last utterance of this sound he produces a quick puff with the breath and thrusts the bag forward as if shooting, which he pretends to do, the missile being supposed to be the invisible sacred mī′gis. The other priests follow in order from the lowest to the highest, each selecting a different joint, during which ordeal the candidate trembles more and more violently until at last he is overcome with the magic influence and falls forward upon the ground unconscious. The Midē′ priests then lay their sacks upon his back, when the candidate begins to recover and spit out the mī′gis shell which he had previously hidden within his mouth. Then the chief Midē′ takes it up between the tips of the forefinger and thumb and goes through the ceremony described in connection with the initiation into the first degree, of holding it toward the east, south, west, north, and the sky, and finally to the mouth of the candidate, when the latter, who has partly recovered from his apparently insensible condition, again relapses into that state. The eight priests then place their sacks to the respective joints at which they previously directed them, which fully infuses the body with the magic influence as desired. Upon this the candidate recovers, takes up the mī′gis shell and, placing it upon his left palm, holds it forward and swings it from side to side, saying he! he! he! he! he! and pretends to swallow it, this time only reeling from its effects. He is now restored to a new life for the second time; and as the priests go to seek seats he is left on the southern side and seats himself. After all those who have been occupied with the initiation have hung up their midē′ sacks on available projections against the wall or branches, the new member goes forward to the pile of tobacco, blankets, and other gifts and divides them among those present, giving the larger portions to the officiating priests. He then passes around once more, stopping before each one to pass his hands over the sides of the priests' heads, and says:

Mi-gwĕtsh′	ga-shi-tō′-win	bi-mâ′-dĭ-si-wĭn
Thanks	for giving to me	life,

after which he retreats a step, and clasping his hands and bowing toward the priest, says:

Ni-ka′-ni	ni-ka′ni	ni-ka′-ni ka-nia′,
fellow midē′	fellow midē′	fellow midē′,

to which each responds hau′, ē. The word hau′ is a term of approbation, ē signifying yes, or affirmation, the two thus used together serving to intensify the expression. Those of the Midē′ present who are of the second, or even some higher degree, then indulge in the ceremony of passing around to the eastern part of the inclosure, where they feign coughing and gagging, so as to produce from the mouth the mī′gis shell, as already narrated in connection with the first degree, p. 192.

This manner of thanking the officiating Midē′ for their services in initiating the candidate into a higher degree is extended also to those members of the Midē′wiwin who are of the first degree only, in acknowledgment of the favor of their presence at the ceremony, they being eligible to attend ceremonial rites of any degree higher than the class to which they belong, because such men are neither benefited nor influenced in any way by merely witnessing such initiation, but they must themselves take the principal part in it to receive the favor of a renewed life and to become possessed of higher power and increased magic influence.

Various members of the society indulge in short harangues, recounting personal exploits in the performance of magic and exorcism, to which the auditors respond in terms of gratification and exclamations of approval. During these recitals the ushers, appointed for the purpose, leave the inclosure by the western door to return in a short time with kettles of food prepared for the midē′ feast. The ushers make four circuits of the interior, giving to each person present a quantity of the contents of the several vessels, so that all receive sufficient to gratify their desires. When the last of the food has been consumed, or removed, the midē′ drum is heard, and soon a song is started, in which all who desire join. After the first two or three verses of the song are recited, a short interval of rest is taken, but when it is resumed dancing begins and is continued to the end. In this manner they indulge in singing and dancing, interspersed with short speeches, until the approach of sunset, when the members retire to their own wig′iwams, leaving the Midē′-wigân by the western egress.

The ushers assisted by the chief Midē′, then remove the sacred post from the inclosure and arrange the interior for new initiations, either of a lower or higher class, if candidates have prepared and presented themselves. In case there is no further need of meeting again at once, the members of the society and visitors return upon the following day to their respective homes.

DESCRIPTIVE NOTES.

The mī′gis shell employed in the second degree initiation is of the same species as those before mentioned. At White Earth, however, some of the priests claim an additional shell as characteristic of this advanced degree, and insist that this should be as nearly round as possible, having a perforation through it by which it may be secured with a strand or sinew. In the absence of a rounded white shell a bead may be used as a substitute. On Pl. XI, No. 4, is presented an illustration of the bead (the second-degree mī′gis) presented to me on the occasion of my initiation.

With reference to the style of facial decoration resorted to in this degree nearly all of the members now paint the face according to their own individual tastes, though a few old men still adhere to the traditional method previously described (pp. 180, 181). The candidate usually adopts the style practiced by his preceptor, to which he is officially entitled; but if the preceptor employed in the preparatory instruction for the second degree be not the same individual whose services were retained for the first time, then the candidate has the privilege of painting his face according to the style of the preceding degree. If he follow his last preceptor it is regarded as an exceptional token of respect, and the student is not expected to follow the method in his further advancement.

A Midē′ of the second degree is also governed by his tutelary daimon; e.g., if during the first fast and vision he saw a bear, he now prepares a necklace of bear-claws, which is worn about the neck and crosses the middle of the breast. He now has the power of changing his form into that of a bear; and during that term of his disguise he wreaks vengeance upon his detractors and upon victims for whose destruction he has been liberally rewarded. Immediately upon the accomplishment of such an act he resumes his human form and thus escapes identification and detection. Such persons are termed by many "bad medicine men," and the practice of thus debasing the sacred teachings of the Midē′wiwin is discountenanced by members of the society generally. Such pretensions are firmly believed in and acknowledged by the credulous and are practiced by that class of Shamans here designated as the Wâbĕnō´.

In his history15 Rev. Mr. Jones says: As the powwows always unite witchcraft with the application of their medicines I shall here give a short account of this curious art.

Witches and wizards are persons supposed to possess the agency of familiar spirits from whom they receive power to inflict diseases on their enemies, prevent good luck of the hunter and the success of the warrior. They are believed to fly invisibly at pleasure from place to place; to turn themselves into bears, wolves, foxes, owls, bats, and snakes. Such metamorphoses they pretend to accomplish by putting on the skins of these animals, at the same time crying and howling in imitation of the creature they wish to represent. Several of our people have informed me that they have seen and heard witches in the shape of these animals, especially the bear and the fox. They say that when a witch in the shape of a bear is being chased all at once she will run round a tree or a hill, so as to be lost sight of for a time by her pursuers, and then, instead of seeing a bear they behold an old woman walking quietly along or digging up roots, and looking as innocent as a lamb. The fox witches are known by the flame of fire which proceeds out of their mouths every time they bark.

Many receive the name of witches without making any pretensions to the art, merely because they are deformed or ill-looking. Persons esteemed witches or wizards are generally eccentric characters, remarkably wicked, of a ragged appearance and forbidding countenance. The way in which they are made is either by direct communication with the familiar spirit during the days of their fasting, or by being instructed by those skilled in the art.

A Midē´ of the second degree has the reputation of superior powers on account of having had the mī´gis placed upon all of his joints, and especially because his heart is filled with magic power, as is shown in Pl. III, No. 48. In this drawing the disk upon the breast denotes where the mī´gis has been "shot" into the figure, the enlarged size of the circle signifying "greater abundance," in contradistinction to the common designation of a mī´gis shown only by a simple spot or small point. One of this class is enabled to hear and see what is transpiring at a remote distance, the lines from the hands indicating that he is enabled to grasp objects which are beyond the reach of a common person, and the lines extending from the feet signifying that he can traverse space and transport himself to the most distant points. Therefore he is sought after by hunters for aid in the discovery and capture of game, for success in war, and for the destruction of enemies, however remote may be their residence.

When an enemy or a rival is to be dealt with a course is pursued similar to that followed when preparing hunting charts, though more powerful magic medicines are used. In the following description of a pictograph recording such an occurrence the Midē´, or rather the Wâbĕnō´, was of the fourth degree of the Midē´wiwin. The indication of the grade of the operator is not a necessary part of the record, but in this instance appears to have been prompted 238 from motives of vanity. The original sketch, of which Fig. 24 is a reproduction, was drawn upon birch-bark by a Midē´, in 1884, and the ceremony detailed actually occurred at White Earth, Minnesota. By a strange coincidence the person against whom vengeance was aimed died of pneumonia the following spring, the disease having resulted from cold contracted during the preceding winter. The victim resided at a camp more than a hundred miles east of the locality above named, and his death was attributed to the Midē´'s power, a reputation naturally procuring for him many new adherents and disciples. The following is the explanation as furnished by a Midē´ familiar with the circumstances:

figure described in text
Fig. 24.—Midē´ destroying an enemy.

No. 1 is the author of the chart, a Midē´ who was called upon to take the life of a man living at a distant camp. The line extending from the midē´ to the figure at No. 9, signifies that his influence will reach to that distance.

No. 2, the applicant for assistance.

Nos. 3, 4, 5, and 6, represent the four degrees of the Midē´wiwin (of which the operator, in this instance, was a member). The degrees are furthermore specifically designated by short vertical strokes.

No. 7 is the midē´ drum used during the ceremony of preparing the charm.

No. 8 represents the body of the intended victim. The heart is indicated, and upon this spot was rubbed a small quantity of vermilion.

No. 9 is the outline of a lake, where the subject operated upon resided.

War parties are not formed at this time, but mnemonic charts of songs used by priests to encourage war parties, are still extant, and a reproduction of one is given on Pl. XIII, D. This song was used by the Midē´ priest to insure success to the parties. The members who intended participating in the exhibition would meet on the evening preceding their departure, and while listening to the words, some would join in the singing while others would dance. The lines may be repeated ad libitum so as to lengthen the entire series of phrases according to the prevalent enthusiasm and the time at the disposal of the performers. The war drum was used, and there were always five or six drummers so as to produce sufficient noise to accord with the loud and animated singing of a large body of excited men. This drum is, in size, like that employed for dancing. It is made by covering with rawhide an old kettle, or wooden vessel, from 2 to 3 feet in diameter. The drum is then attached to four sticks, or short posts, so as to prevent its touching the ground, thus affording every advantage for producing full and resonant sounds, when struck. The drumsticks are strong withes, at the end of each of which is fastened a ball of buckskin thongs. The following lines are repeated ad libitum: 239

mnemonic song
Plate XIII.d. Mnemonic Song.
Hu´-na-wa´-na ha´-wä, un-do´-

line drawing
    dzhe-na′ ha-we′-nĕ.
    I am looking [feeling] for my paint.
    [The Midē's hands are at his medicine sack searching for his war paint.]

line drawing
    Hīa′-dzhi-mĭn-de′ non′-da-kō′,
    They hear me speak of legs.
    Refers to speed in the expedition. To the left of the leg is the arm of a spirit, which is supposed to infuse magic influence so as to give speed and strength.

line drawing
    Hu′-wa-ke′, na′, ha′,
    He said,
    The Turtle Man′idō will lend his aid in speed. The turtle was one of the swiftest man′idōs, until through some misconduct, Min′abō′zho deprived him of his speed.

line drawing
    Wa′-tshe, ha′, hwē, wa′-ka-te′, hē′, wa′-tshe, ha′, hwē′.
    Powder, he said.
    [The modern form of Wa′-ka-te′, he′, hwā′, is ma′-ka-dē′-hwa; other archaic words occur also in other portions of this song. The phrase signifies that the Midē′ Man′idō favors good results from the use of powder. His form projects from the top of the Midē′ structure.]

vertical lines
    Rest. A smoke is indulged in after which the song is resumed, accompanied with dancing.

line drawing
    Sin-go′-na wa-kī′ na-ha′-ka
    I made him cry.
    The figure is that of a turkey buzzard which the speaker shot.

line drawing
    Te-wa′-tshi-me-kwe′-na, ha′, na-ke′-nan.
    They tell of my powers.
    The people speak highly of the singer's magic powers; a charmed arrow is shown which terminates above with feather-web ornament, enlarged to signify its greater power.

He′-wĕ-ne-nis′-sa ma-he′-ka-

line drawing
    nĕn′-na.
    What have I killed, it is a wolf.
    By aid of his magic influence the speaker has destroyed a bad man′idō which had assumed the form of a wolf.

line drawing
    Sam-gu-we′-wa, ha′, nīn-dēn′, tshi′-man-da′-kwa ha′na-nĭn-dēn′.
    I am as strong as the bear.
    The Midē′ likens his powers to those of the Bear Man′idō, one of the most powerful spirits; his figure protrudes from the top of the Midē′wigân while his spirit form is indicated by the short lines upon the back.

240 Wa′-ka-na′-ni, hē′, wa′-ka-na′-ni.

line drawing
    I wish to smoke.
    The pipe used is that furnished by the promoter or originator of the war party, termed a "partisan." The Midē′ is in full accord with the work undertaken and desires to join, signifying his wish by desiring to smoke with the braves.

line drawing
    He′-wa-hō′-a hai′-a-nē′
    I even use a wooden image.
    Effigies made to represent one who is to be destroyed. The heart is punctured, vermilion or other magic powder is applied, and the death of the victim is encompassed.

line drawing
    Pa-kwa′ na-ko-nē′ ā′, ō′, hē′, nĕh-ke′-na-ko-nē′-a.
    The bear goes round angry.
    [The Bear Man′idō is angry because the braves are dilatory in going to war. The sooner they decide upon this course, the better it will be for the Midē′ as to his fee, and the chances of success are greater while the braves are infused with enthusiasm, than if they should become sluggish and their ardor become subdued.]

THIRD DEGREE.

midewigan as described in text
    Fig. 25. —Diagram of Midē′wigân of the third degree.

The structure in which the third degree of the Midē′wiwin is conferred resembles that of the two preceding, and an outline is presented in Fig. 25. In this degree three posts are erected, the first one resembling that of the first degree, being painted red with a band of green around the top. (Pl. XV, No. 1.) This is planted a short distance to the east of the middle of the floor. The second post is also painted red, but has scattered over its entire surface spots of white clay, each of about the size of a silver quarter of a dollar, symbolical of the mī′gis shell. Upon the top of this post is placed the stuffed body of an owl—Kŏ-kó-kŏ-ō′. (Pl. XV, No. 2.) This post is planted a short distance west of the first one and about midway between it and the third, which last is erected within about 6 or 8 feet from the western door, and is painted black. (Pl. XV, No. 3.) The sacred stone against which patients are placed, and which has the alleged virtue of removing or expelling the demons that cause disease, is placed upon the ground at the usual spot near the eastern entrance (Fig. 25, No. 1). The Makwá Man′idō—bear spirit—is the tutelary guardian of this degree. Cedar trees are planted at each of the outer angles of the structure (Fig. 25, Nos. 6, 7, 8, 9). The sudatory is erected about 100 yards due east of the main entrance of the Midē′wigân, and is of the same size and for the same purpose as that for the second degree.

sacred posts
    Plate XV. Sacred Posts Of Midē′wigân.
24

PREPARATION OF CANDIDATE.

It is customary for the period of one year to elapse before a second-degree Midē′ can be promoted, even if he be provided with enough presents for such advancement. As the exacted fee consists of goods and tobacco thrice the value of the fee for the first degree, few present themselves. This degree is not held in as high estimation, relatively, as the preceding one; but it is alleged that a Midē´'s powers are intensified by again subjecting himself to the ceremony of being "shot with the sacred mī´gis," and he is also elevated to that rank by means of which he may be enabled the better to invoke the assistance of the tutelary guardian of this degree.

A Midē´ who has in all respects complied with the preliminaries of announcing to the chief Midē´ his purpose, gaining satisfactory evidence of his resources and ability to present the necessary presents, and of his proficiency in the practice of medical magic, etc., selects a preceptor of at least the third degree and one who is held in high repute and influence in the Midē´wiwin. After procuring the services of such a person and making a satisfactory agreement with him, he may be enabled to purchase from him some special formulæ for which he is distinguished. The instruction embraces a résumé of the traditions previously given, the various uses and properties of magic plants and compounds with which the preceptor is familiar, and conversations relative to exploits performed in medication, incantation, and exorcism. Sometimes the candidate is enabled to acquire new "medicines" to add to his list, and the following is a translation of the tradition relating to the origin of ginseng (Aralia quinquefolia, Gr.), the so-called "man root," held in high estimation as of divine origin. In Fig. 3 is presented a pictorial representation of the story, made by Ojibwa, a Midē´ priest of White Earth, Minnesota. The tradition purports to be an account of a visit of the spirit of a boy to the abode of Dzhibai´-Man´idō, "the chief spirit of the place of souls," called Ne´-ba-gi´-zis, "the land of the sleeping sun."

figure described in text
Fig. 3. —Origin of Ginseng.
Larger Figure

There appears to be some similarity between this tradition and that given in connection with Pl. V , in which the Sun Spirit restored to life a boy, by which act he exemplified a portion of the ritual of the Midē´wiwin. It is probable therefore that the following tradition is a corruption of the former and made to account for the origin of "man root," as ginseng is designated, this root, or certain portions of it, being so extensively employed in various painful complaints. Once an old Midē´, with his wife and son, started out on a hunting trip, and, as the autumn was changing into winter, the three erected a substantial wig´iwam. The snow began to fall and the cold increased, so they decided to remain and eat of their stores, game having been abundant and a good supply having been procured. 242 The son died; whereupon his mother immediately set out for the village to obtain help to restore him to life, as she believed her father, the chief priest of the Midē´-wiwin, able to accomplish this.

When the woman informed her father of the death of her son, her brother, who was present, immediately set out in advance to render assistance. The chief priest then summoned three assistant Midē´, and they accompanied his daughter to the place where the body of his dead grandson lay upon the floor of the wig´iwam, covered with robes.

The chief Midē´ placed himself at the left shoulder of the dead boy, the next in rank at the right, while the two other assistants stationed themselves at the feet. Then the youngest Midē´—he at the right foot of the deceased—began to chant a midē´ song, which he repeated a second, a third, and a fourth time.

When he had finished, the Midē´ at the left foot sang a midē´ song four times; then the Midē´ at the right shoulder of the body did the same, after which the chief Midē´ priest sang his song four times, whereupon there was a perceptible movement under the blanket, and as the limbs began to move the blanket was taken off, when the boy sat up. Being unable to speak, he made signs that he desired water, which was given to him.

The four Midē´ priests then chanted medicine songs, each preparing charmed remedies which were given to the boy to complete his recovery. The youngest Midē´, standing at the foot of the patient, gave him four pinches of powder, which he was made to swallow; the Midē´ at the left foot did the same; then the Midē´ at the right shoulder did likewise, and he, in turn, was followed by the chief priest standing at the left shoulder of the boy; whereupon the convalescent immediately recovered his speech and said that during the time that his body had been in a trance his spirit had been in the "spirit land," and had learned of the "grand medicine."

The boy then narrated what his spirit had experienced during the trance, as follows: "Gi´-gi-min´-ĕ-go´-min midē´-wi-wĭn mi-dē´ man´-i-dō´ B 'n-gigĭn´-o-a-mâk ban-dzhi´-ge´-o-we´-ân ta´-zi-ne´-zho-wak´ ni-zha´-nĕ-zak, kĭwi´-de-gĕt mi´-o-pi´-ke´-ne-bŭi´-yan ka-ki´-nĕ ka-we´-dĕ-ge´ mi´-o-wŏk-pi´ i-kan´-o-a-mag´-ĭ-na mi-dē´ man´i-dō wi-we´-ni-tshi mi-dē´-wi-wĭn, ki´-mimâ´-dĭ-si-win´-in-ân´ ki-mi´-nĭ-go-nan´ ge-on´-dĕ-na-mŏngk ki´-mi-mâ´-di-si´-wa-in-an´; ki´-ki-no´-a-mag´-wi-nan´ mash´-kĭ-ki o-gi´-mi-ni´-go-wan´ odzhi-bi´-gân gi-me´-ni-na-gŭk´ mash´-kĭ-ki-wa´-bo shtĭk-wan´-a-ko-se´-an oma´-mâsh´-kĭ-ki ma´-gi-ga´-to ki´-kaya-tōn."

The following is a translation:

"He, the chief spirit of the Midē´ Society, gave us the "grand medicine," and he has taught us how to use it. I have come back from the spirit land. There will be twelve, all of whom will take wives; when the last of these is no longer without a wife, then will I die. That is the time. The Midē´ spirit taught us to do right. He gave us life and told us how to prolong it. These things he taught us, and gave us roots for medicine. I give to you medicine; if your head is sick, this medicine put upon it, you will put it on."

The revelation received by the boy was in the above manner imparted to the Indians. The reference to twelve—three times the sacred number four—signifies that twelve chief priests shall succeed each other before death will come to the narrator. It is observed, also, that a number of the words are archaic, which fact appears to be an indication of some antiquity, at least, of the tradition.

The following are the principal forms in which a Midē′ will utilize Aralia quinquefolia, Gr., ginseng—Shtĕ′-nabi-o′-dzhi-bik:

243

1. Small quantities of powdered root are swallowed to relieve stomachic pains.

2. A person complaining with acute pains in any specific part of the body is given that part of the root corresponding to the part affected; e.g., for pleurisy, the side of the root is cut out, and an infusion given to relieve such pains; if one has pains in the lower extremities, the bifurcations of the root are employed; should the pains be in the thorax, the upper part of the root—corresponding to the chest—is used in a similar manner.

INITIATION OF CANDIDATE.

As the candidate for promotion has acquired from his Midē′ friends such new information as they choose to impart, and from his instructor all that was practicable, he has only to await the day of ceremony to be publicly acknowledged as a third-degree Midē′. As this time approaches the invitation sticks are sent to the various members and to such nonresident Midē′ as the officiating priests may wish to honor. On or before the fifth day previous to the meeting the candidate moves to the vicinity of the Midē′wigân. On that day the first sweat bath is taken, and one also upon each succeeding day until four baths, as a ceremony of purification, have been indulged in. On the evening of the day before the meeting his preceptor visits him at his own wig′iwam when, with the assistance of friends, the presents are collected and carried to the Midē′-wigân and suspended from the transverse poles near the roof. The officiating priests may subsequently join him, when smoking and singing form the chief entertainment of the evening.

By this time numerous visitors have gathered together and are encamped throughout the adjacent timber, and the sound of the drum, where dancing is going on, may be heard far into the night.

Early on the morning of the day of the ceremonies the candidate goes to the sudatory where he first awaits the coming of his preceptor and later the arrival of the Midē′ priests by whom he is escorted to the Midē′wigân. With the assistance of the preceptor he arranges his gift of tobacco which he takes with him to the sacred inclosure, after which a smoke offering is made, and later Midē′ songs are chanted. These may be of his own composition as he has been a professor of magic a sufficient lapse of time to have composed them, but to give evidence of superior powers the chief, or some other of the officiating priests, will perhaps be sufficiently inspired to sing. The following was prepared and chanted by one of the Midē′ priests at the third-degree meeting at White Earth, Minnesota, and the illustration in Pl. XIV, A, is a reproduction of the original. The words, with translation, are as follows:

mnemonic song
Plate XIVa. Mnemonic Song.

line drawing Ni-ka′-ni-na man′-do-na-mō′-a.

My friend I am shooting into you in trying to hit the mark.

[The two arms are grasping the mī′gis, which he the Midē′ is going to shoot into the body of the candidate. The last word means, literally, trying to hit the mark at random.]

244 Me-kwa′-me-sha-kwak′, mi-tē′-wi-da′.

line drawing While it is clear let us have it, the "grand medicine."

The Midē′ arm, signified by the magic zigzag lines at the lower end of the picture, reaches up into the sky to keep it clear; the rain is descending elsewhere as indicated by the lines descending from the sky at the right and left.

vertical lines Rest.

During this interval a smoke offering is made.

line drawing Mi-sha′-kwi-tō- mī′-gĭs-sĭm′.

As clear as the sky [is] my mī′gis.

The figure represents the sacred mī′gis, as indicated by the short lines radiating from the periphery. The mī′gis is white and the clear sky is compared to it.

line drawing Sōn′-gi-mi-dē′ wi-ka′-ne, hē′, Wi-nō′-a man′-i-dō′-wi-dzhī′-id-e′-zhi-wât.

Take the "grand medicine" strong, as they, together with the "Great Spirit," tell me.

[The candidate is enjoined to persevere in his purpose. The associate Midē′ are alluded to, as also Ki′tshi Man′idō, who urge his continuance and advancement in the sacred society. The arm reaches down to search for the sacred mī′gis of the fourth degree—designated by four vertical lines—which is, as yet, hidden from the person addressed.]

line drawing Hwa′-ba-mi-dē′, hwa′-ba-mi-dē′, Na′-wa-kin-tē′.

He who sees me, he who sees me, stands on the middle of the earth.

[The human figure symbolizes Ki′tshi Man′idō; the magic lines cross his body, while his legs rest upon the outline of the Midē′wigân. His realm, the sky, reaches from the zenith to the earth, and he beholds the Midē′ while chanting and conducting the Midē′wiwin.]

line drawing Man′i-dō′ wi′-ka-ni′ ni-mi-dē′.

To the spirit be a friend, my Midē′.

The speaker enjoins the candidate to be faithful to his charge, and thus a friend to Ki′tshi Man′idō, who in return will always assist him. The figure holds a mī′gis in its right hand, and the Midē′ drum in its left.

The greater number of words in the preceding text are of an archaic form, and are presented as they were chanted. The several lines may be repeated ad libitum to accord with the feeling of inspiration which the singer experiences, or the amount of interest manifested by his hearers.

All the members of the society not officially inducting the candidate have ere this entered the Midē′wigân and deposited their invitation sticks near the sacred stone, or, in the event of their inability 245 to attend, have sent them with an explanation. The candidate, at the suggestion of the Midē′ priest, then prepares to leave the sudatory, gathers up the tobacco, and as he slowly advances toward the Midē′ inclosure his attendants fall into the procession according to their office. The priests sing as they go forward, until they reach the entrance of the Midē′wigân, where the candidate and his preceptor halt, while the remainder enter and take their stations just within the door, facing the west.

The drummers, who are seated in the southwestern angle of the inclosure, begin to drum and sing, while the candidate is led slowly around the exterior, going by the south, thus following the course of the sun. Upon the completion of the fourth circuit he is halted directly opposite the main entrance, to which his attention is then directed. The drumming and singing cease; the candidate beholds two Midē′ near the outer entrance and either side of it. These Midē′ represent two malevolent man′idō and guard the door against the entrance of those not duly prepared. The one upon the northern side of the entrance then addresses his companion in the following words: I′-ku-tan ka′-wi-nad′-gĭ wa′-na-mâ′-sĭ ē′-zhĭ-gĭ′-nĭ-gĕd—"Do you not see how he is formed?" To which the other responds: O-da′-pĭ-nō′ ke′-no-wĭn-dŭng shkwan′-dĭm—"Take care of it, the door;" [i.e., guard the entrance.] The former then again speaks to his companion, and says: Ka-wīn′-nĭ-na-ga′ wâ′-ba-ma′-sĭ-ba′-shī′-gĭ′-ne-gēt′—"Do you not see how he carries the goods?" The Midē′ spoken to assents to this, when the preceptor takes several pieces of tobacco which he presents to the two guards, whereupon they permit the candidate to advance to the inner entrance, where he is again stopped by two other guardian man′idō,

who turn upon him as if to inquire the reason of his intrusion. The candidate then holds out two parcels of tobacco and says to them: O-da′-pin a-sē′-ma—"Take it, the tobacco," whereupon they receive the gift and stand aside, saying: Kun′-da-dan—"Go down;" [i.e., enter and follow the path.] As the candidate is taken a few steps forward and toward the sacred stone, four of the eight officiating priests receive him, one replacing the preceptor who goes to the extreme western end there to stand and face the east, where another joins him, while the remaining two place themselves side by side so as to face the west.

It is believed that there are five powerful man′idōs who abide within the third-degree Midē′wigân, one of whom is the Midē′ man′idō—Ki′tshi Man′idō—one being present at the sacred stone, the second at that part of the ground between the sacred stone and the first part where the gifts are deposited, the remaining three at the three degree posts.

As the candidate starts and continues upon his walk around the interior of the inclosure the musicians begin to sing and drum, while all those remaining are led toward the left, and when opposite the 246 sacred stone he faces it and is turned round so that his back is not toward it in passing; the same is done at the second place where one of the spirits is supposed to abide; again at first, second, and third posts. By this time the candidate is at the western extremity of the structure, and as the second Midē′ receives him in charge, the other taking his station beside the preceptor, he continues his course toward the north and east to the point of departure, going through similar evolutions as before, as he passes the three posts, the place of gifts and the sacred stone. This is done as an act of reverence to the man′idōs and to acknowledge his gratitude for their presence and encouragement. When he again arrives at the eastern extremity of the inclosure he is placed between the two officiating Midē′, who have been awaiting his return, while his companion goes farther back, even to the door, from which point he addresses

the other officiating Midē′ as follows:

Mĭs-sa′-a-shi′-gwa	wi-kan′-da′-we-an′,	mĭs-sa′-a-shi′-gwa
Now is the time	[I am] telling [—advising,]	now is the time
wī′-di-wa′-mŏk to be observed	wi-un′-o-bē-ŏg. [I am] ready to make him sit down.	

Then one of the Midē′ priests standing beside the candidate leads him to the spot between the sacred stone and the first-degree post where the blankets and other goods have been deposited, and here he is seated. This priest then walks slowly around him singing in a tremulous manner wa′, hē′, hē′, hē′, hē′, hē′, hē′, hē′, returning to a position so as to face him, when he addresses him as follows: Mĭs-sa′-a-shi′-gwa pŏ′-gŭ-sē-ni′-mi-nan′ au′-u-sa′ za-a′-da-win′ man′-i-dō mī′-gis. Na′-pish-gatsh di-mâ′-gĭ-sĭ ĕ-nĕ′-nĭ-mi-an pi′-sha-gâ-an-da-i′ na′-pish-gatsh tshi-skwa′-di-na-wâd′ dzhi-ma′-dzhi-a-ka′-ma-da-mân bi-mâ′-dĭs-si′-an.

The following is a free translation: The time has arrived for you to ask of the Great Spirit this "reverence" i.e., the sanctity of this degree. I am interceding in your behalf, but you think my powers are feeble; I am asking him to confer upon you the sacred powers. He may cause many to die, but I shall henceforth watch your course of success in life, and learn if he will heed your prayers and recognize your magic power.

At the conclusion of these remarks three others of the officiating Midē′ advance and seat themselves, with their chief, before the candidate. The Midē′ drum is handed to the chief priest, and after a short prelude of drumming he becomes more and more inspired, and sings the following Midē′ song, represented pictorially, also on Pl. XIV , B .

mnemonic song
    Plate XIV.b. Mnemonic Song.
line Man′-i-dō′ we-da′, man′-i-dō′ draw-gi-dō′ we-do′-nĭng.
ing   Let us be a spirit, let the spirit come from the mouth.
    The head is said to signify

247 Nin´-de-wen´-don zha´-bon-děsh´-kâ-mân´.

In this lodge, through which I pass.

The speaker claims that he has been received into the degree of the Midē´wiwin to which he refers. The objects on the outer side of the oblong square character represent spirits, those of the bear.

Ân´-dzhe-ho ĭ´-a-ni´ o-gēn´, ingē´-ō-ke´, hwe´-ō-ke´.

Mother is having it over again.

The reference is to the earth, as having the ceremony of the "grand medicine" again.

Ni´-ka-nan ni´-go-sân, ni´-go-sân, ni-ka´-ni-san´, man´-i-dō´ wi-dzhig´ nin-go-sân´ an-i-wa´-bi-dzhig ni-ka´.

Friends I am afraid, I am afraid, friends, of the spirits sitting around me.

[The speaker reaches his hand toward the sky, i.e., places his faith in Ki´tshi Man´idō who abides above.]

Ya´-ki-no´-sha-me´-wa, ya´-ki-no´-sha-me´-wa, ya-ki-no-si-ka-ne, ya-ki-no-si-ka-ne, hē´, ki´-no-sha´-we-wa´.

I am going, with medicine bag, to the lodge.

[The object represents an otter skin Midē´ sack, the property of the speaker.]

Ya´-be-kai´-a-bi, ya´-be-kai´-a-bi, hē´-ā´, hē´-ā´, ya´-be-kai´-a-bi, ya´-be-kai´-a-bi, hē´-ā´, hē´-ā´, wa´-na-he´-ni´-o-ni´, ya´-be-kai´-o-bik´.

We are still sitting in a circle.

[A Midē´ sitting within the Midē´wigân; the circle is shown.]

A-ya´-a-bi-ta´ pa´-ke-zhĭk´, ū´, hū´, a´,

Half the sky

The hand is shown reaching toward the sky, imploring the assistance of Ki´tshi Man´idō that the candidate may receive advancement in power. He has only two degrees, one-half of the number desired.

Baw´-be-ke´ o´-gi-mân nish´-a-we, hē´, ne´-me-ke-hē´, nish´-a-we´-ni-mĭk o´-gi-mân.

The spirit has pity on me now.

[The "Great Spirit" is descending upon the Midē´wigân, to be present during the ceremony.]

Nin-dai´-a, nin-dai´-a, ha´, we´-ki-ma´, ha´, wâ-no-kwe´.

In my heart, in my heart, I have the spirit.

[The hand is holding the mī´gis, to which reference is made.]

Ikw-u-ha´-ma man-ta-na´-ki-na ni-ka´-ni

I take the earth, my Midē´ friends.

The earth furnishes the resources necessary to the maintenance of life, both food and medicines.

248 Wi´-a-ya´-din shin-da´, hân´, man-da´-ha-ni´, o-hō´ ni-bĭ´.

Let us get him to take this water.

[The figure sees medicine in the earth, as the lines from the eyes to the horizontal strokes indicate.]

Hŭe´-shī´-shi-kwa´-ni-an nin-ga´-ga-mūn´.

I take this rattle.

The rattle is used when administering medicine.

Wi-wa´-ba-mi´na hē´-na ko´-ni-a´-ni, ka´, ko-ni-a´-ho-nā´, nī´, kā´.

See how I shine in making medicine.

[The speaker likens himself to the Makwa´ Man´idō, one of the most powerful Midē´ spirits. His body shines as if it were ablaze with light—due to magic power.]

This song is sung ad libitum according to the inspired condition of the person singing it. Many of the words are archaic, and differ from the modern forms.

Then the officiating priests arise and the one lowest in rank grasps his Midē´ sack and goes through the gestures, described in connection with the previous degrees, of shooting into the joints and forehead of the candidate the sacred mī´gis. At the attempt made by the chief priest the candidate falls forward apparently unconscious. The priests then touch his joints and forehead with the upper end of their Midē´ sacks whereupon he recovers and rises to a standing posture. The chief then addresses him and enjoins him to conduct himself with propriety and in accordance with the dignity of his profession. The following is the text, viz: Gi-gan´-bis-sīn dau´-gē-in´-ni-nân´ kish-bin´-bish-in dau´-o-ân-nīn da´-ki-ka-wa´-bi-kwe ga´-kĭ-ne ke-ke´-wi-bi´-na-mōn ki-ma´-dzhĭ-zhi we´-bĭ-zi-wĭn´.

The translation is as follows: "You heed to what I say to you; if you are listening and will do what is right you will live to have white hair. That is all; you will do away with all bad actions."

The Midē´ priest second in rank then says to the candidate: Ke´-go-wi´-ka-za´-gi-to-wa´-kin ki-da´-no-ka´tshĭ-gân kai-ē´-gi-gīt´ a-sē´-ma, kai´-e-mī´-dzĭm, which signifies: "Never begrudge your goods, neither your tobacco, nor your provisions." To this the candidate responds ē´—yes, by this signifying that he will never regret what he has given the Midē´ for their services. The candidate remains standing while the members of the society take seats, after which he goes to the pile of blankets, skins, and other presents, and upon selecting appropriate ones for the officiating priests he carries them to those persons, after which he makes presents of less value to all other Midē´ present. Tobacco is then distributed, and while all are preparing to make an offering to Ki´tshi Man´idō of tobacco, the 249 newly accepted member goes around to each, member present, passes his hands downward over the sides of the Midē's head and says:

Mi- gwĕtsh´	ga-shi-tō´- win	bi-ma´-dĭ-si- wīn´,
Thanks	for giving to me	life,

then, stepping back, he clasps his hands and bows toward the Midē´, adding: Ni-ka´-ni, ni-ka´-ni, ni-ka´-ni, ka-na´,— "My Midē´ friend, my Midē´ friend, my Midē´ friend, friend." To this the Midē´ responds in affirmation, hau´, ē´—yes.

The new member then finds a seat on the southern side of the inclosure, whereupon the ushers—Midē´ appointed to attend to outside duties—retire and bring in the vessels of food which are carried around to various persons present, four distinct times.

The feast continues for a considerable length of time, after which the kettles and dishes are again carried outside the Midē´wi-gân, when all who desire indulge in smoking. Midē´ songs are chanted by one of the priests, the accompanying, reproduced pictorially in Pl. XIV C, being an example. The lines, as usual, are repeated ad libitum, the music being limited to but few notes, and in a minor key. The following are the words with translation:

mnemonic song
Plate XIV.c. Mnemonic Song.

line drawing He´-ne-wi´-a na mi´-si-man´-i-dē-ge´
Their bodies shine over the world
he-wa´-we-a´-ne-kan´.
unto me as unto you, my Midē´ friend.
This refers to the sun, and moon, whose bodies are united in the drawing.

line drawing Ma´-na-wi-na´ hai´-e-ne-hā´ be-wa´-bik-kun
Your eyes see them both
eyes made of iron,
kan-din´-a-we.
piercing eyes.
The figure is that of the crane, whose loud, far-reaching voice is indicated by the short lines radiating from the mouth. The eyes of the crane Man´idō are equally penetrating.

line drawing he-shi-be´-nĕ-wa´ ma´-si-ni´-ni-wa´, hā´ he´-shi-wa´, hā´.
Calm it leads you to guides you to your food.
Knowledge of superior powers gained through familiarity with the rites of the Midē´wiwin is here referred to. The figure points to the abode of Ki´tshi Man´idō; three short lines indicating three degrees in the Midē´wiwin, which the candidate has taken.

line drawing Ha-nin´-di bik´-kĭn-he´ he- man´- ni-i-dō kan´
Whence does he rise spirit from the mide´ Midē´ friend from the east.
wa-ba-nŭnk´, mi-dē´-man´-i-dō wa-ba-nŭnk´.
from the east, man´ido
[The hand reaches up as in making the gesture for rising sun or day, the "sky lines" leaning to the left, or east; one making signs is always presumed to face the south, and signs referring to periods of day, sun, sunrise, etc., are made from the left side of the body.]
250 Rest.

vertical lines
line drawing Wa-dzhi-wan´, wa-dzhi-wan´-na,
Wa-dahi-wan´ ni-ka´-na-hē´.
There is a mountain, there is a mountain,
There is a mountain, my friends.
[The upright outline represents a mountain upon which a powerful Midē´ is seated, symbolical of the distinction attainable by a Midē´.]

line drawing Wa´-bĕ-kŭ-ĕ-be-a´, na´-bĕ-kŭ-ĕ-be-a´ wa´-bĕ-kŭ-ĕ-be-a´, man´-i-dō´-´a man´-i-dō´-a nin-dē´.
Shot it was, and it hit body, your man´ido shot it was man´ido your heart. your heart. nin-dē´.
[The Mī´gis is represented in the illustration by the small rings; the arrow indicating that it was "shot" with velocity.]

line drawing
line drawing
Hwe´-kwo-nin´-na-ta, ki-wī´-kash´-ka-man;
En-do´-ge-mā´ wesh´-in-ē´.
What am I going around?
I am going around the Midē´wigân.
[The oblong structure represents the Midē´wigân. The otter-skin Midē´ sack is taken around it, as is shown by the outline of that animal and the line or course indicated. The Makwa´ Man´idō (bear spirit) is shown at the left, resting upon the horizontal line, the earth, below which are magic lines showing his power, as also the lines upon the back of the bear. The speaker compares himself to the bear spirit.]

line drawing Nen´-do-ne´-ha-mān-ni´ nī´-ŏ,
What am I looking at.
The figure denotes a leg, signifying powers of transporting one's self to remote places; the magic power is indicated by the three transverse lines and the small spots, the mī´gis, upon it.

line drawing Ba´ke-en non´-do-wa-wē´, hī´,
I soon heard him, the one who did not listen to them.
[The Midē´, as a superior personage, is shown by having the horns attached to the head. The line of hearing has small rings,

line drawing
pī´-na-nī´, hin´-ta-na´-wi ni-ka´-na-ga´ na´-ge-ka-na´ ē´, hē´.

ᕽwi-tg-na´-wi ni-ka´-na-gi´, ē´, hē´,

The Nika´ni are finding fault with me, inside of my lodge.

[The arm at the side of the Midē´wigân points to the interior, the place spoken of.]

251 Osh´-kosh-na-nā´ pi-na´-wa ni-bosh´-i-na´-na.

line drawing

With the bear's claws I almost hit him.

The Midē´ used the bear's claw to work a charm, or exorcism, and would seem to indicate that he claimed the powers of a Wâbĕnō´. The one spoken of is an evil man´idō, referred to in the preceding line, in which he speaks of having heard him.

At the conclusion of this protracted ceremony a few speeches may be made by a Midē´, recounting the benefits to be enjoyed and the powers wielded by the knowledge thus acquired, after which the chief priest intimates to his colleagues the advisability of adjourning. They then leave the Midē´wigân by the western door, and before night all movable accessories are taken away from the structure.

The remainder of the evening is spent in visiting friends, dancing, etc., and upon the following day they all return to their respective homes.

DESCRIPTIVE NOTES.

Although the mī´gis shell of the several degrees is generally of the same species, some of the older Midē´ priests claim that there were formerly specific shells, each being characteristic and pertaining specially to each individual grade. The objects claimed by Sika´s-sigĕ as referring to the third degree are, in addition to the Cypræa monata, L., a piece of purple wampum, and one shell of elongated form, both shown on Pl. XI, Nos. 3 and 5, respectively.

The fact of a Midē´ having been subjected to "mī´gis shooting" for the third time is an all-sufficient reason to the Indian why his powers are in a corresponding manner augmented. His powers of exorcism and incantation are greater; his knowledge and use of magic medicines more extended and certain of effect; and his ability to do harm, as in the capacity of a Wâbĕnō´, is more and more lauded and feared. He becomes possessed of a greater power in prophecy and prevision, and in this state enters the class of personages known as the Jĕs´sakkīd´, or jugglers. His power over darkness and obscurity is indicated on Pl. III, A, No. 77, upon which the head, chest, and arms are represented as being covered with lines to designate obscurity, the extended arms with outstretched hands denoting ability to grasp and control that which is hidden to the eye.

juggler's lodge

Fig. 26. —Jĕs´sakkân´ or juggler's lodge.

The Jĕs´sakkīd´ and his manner of performing have already been mentioned. This class of sorcerers were met with by the Jesuit Fathers early in the seventeenth century, and referred to under various designations, such as jongleur, magicien, consulteur du manitou, etc. Their influence in the tribe was recognized, and formed one of the greatest obstacles encountered in the Christianization of the Indians. Although the Jĕs´sakkīd´ may be a seer and prophet as well as a practitioner of exorcism without becoming a 252 member of the Midē´wiwin, it is only when a Midē´ attains the rank of the third degree that he begins to give evidence of, or pretends to exhibit with any degree of confidence, the powers accredited to the former. The structure erected and occupied by the Jĕs´sakkīd´ for the performance of his powers as prophet or oracle has before been described as cylindrical, being made by planting four or more poles and wrapping about them sheets of birch bark, blankets, or similar material that will serve as a covering. This form of structure is generally represented in pictographic records, as shown in Fig. 26.

juggler's lodge

juggler's lodge

Fig. 27. — Jĕs´sakkân´, or juggler's lodge.

Fig. 28. — Jĕs´sakkân´, or juggler's lodge.

juggler's lodge

Fig. 29. —Jĕs´sakkân´, juggler's lodge.

The accompanying illustrations, Figs. 27, 28, and 29, reproduced from birchbark etchings, were the property of Jĕs´sakkīd´, who were also Midē´ of the third and fourth degrees. It will be noticed that the structure used by them is in the form of the ordinary wig´iwam, as their profession of medical magic is apparently held in higher esteem than the art of prophecy; their status and claims as Jĕs´sakkīd´ being indicated by the great number of ma´nidōs which they have the power of invoking. These man´idōs, or spirits, are indicated by the outline of their material forms, the heart being indicated and connected with the interior of the structure to show the power of the Jĕs´sakkīd´ over the life of the respective spirits. The Thunderbird usually occupies the highest position in his estimation, and for this reason is drawn directly over the wig´iwam. The Turtle is claimed to be the man´idō who acts as intermediary between the Jĕs´sakkīd´ and the other man´idōs, and is therefore not found among the characters on the outside of the wig´iwam, but his presence is indicated within, either at the spot marking the convergence of the "life lines," or immediately below it.

juggler's lodge

Fig. 30. — Jĕs´sakkân´ or juggler's lodge. Fig. 30 is a reproduction of an 253 etching made by a Jĕs´sakkīd´ at White Earth, Minnesota. The two curved lines above the Jĕs´sakkan´ represent the sky, from which magic power is derived, as shown by the waving line extending downward. The small spots within the structure are "magic spots," i.e., the presence of man´idōs. The juggler is shown upon the left side near the base.

When a prophet is so fortunate as to be able to claim one of these man´idōs as his own tutelary daimon, his advantage in invoking the others is comparatively greater. Before proceeding to the Jĕs´sakkân—or the "Jugglery," as the Jĕs´sakkīd´ wig´iwam is commonly designated, a prophet will prepare himself by smoking and making an offering to his man´idō, and by singing a chant, of which an example is presented on Pl. XIV, D. It is a reproduction of one made by a Jĕs´sakkīd´ who was also a Midē´ of the third degree. Each line is chanted as often as may be desired, or according to the effect which it may be desirable to produce or the inspired state of the singer.

mnemonic song
Plate XIV.d. Mnemonic Song.

line drawing Me-ing´-yan, ha´, ha´, ha´,
I go into the Jĕs´sakkan´ to see the medicine.
The circle represents the Jĕs´sakkīd´ as viewed from above; the short lines denote the magic character of the structure, and the central ring, or spot, the magic stone used by the prophet who appears entering from the side.

line drawing Sa-nun´-dōn´, he´, he´, he´, he´,
I was the one who dug up life.
The Otter Man´idō emerging from the Midē´wigân; he received it from Ki´tshi Mani´dō.

line drawing Ni´ka-nī´ we-do-ko´-a, ha´, ha´,
The spirit put down medicine on earth to grow.
The sacred or magic lines descending to the earth denote supernatural origin of the mī´gis, which is shown by the four small rings. The short lines at the bottom represent the ascending sprouts of magic plants.

line drawing Ta-ti-ba´-tshi mŭt´-â-wit´, tē´, hē´, hē´,
I am the one that dug up the medicine.
The otter shown emerging from the jugglery. The speaker represents himself "like unto the Otter Man´idō."

line drawing Ki´wa-win´-da ma´-kwa-nan´, na´, ha´,
I answer my brother spirit.
The Otter Man´idō responds to the invocation of the speaker. The diagonal line across the body signifies the "spirit character" of the animal.

254 Rest or pause.

vertical lines

line drawing Wa-ing so´-at wĕn´-ti´-na-man, ha´, ha
The spirit has put life into my body.
The speaker is represented as being in the Midē´-wigân, where Ki´tshi Man´idō placed magic power into his body; the arms denote this act of putting into his sides the mī´gis. The line crossing the body denotes the person to be possessed of supernatural power.

line drawing Kiwin na-bi´-in, nē´, hē´, hē´,
This is what the medicine has given us.
The Midē´wigân, showing on the upper line the guardian man´idōs.

line drawing Ni-wi-she-we´-ni-bĭ-ku´, hū´, hū´, hē´,
I took with two hands what was thrown down to us.
The speaker grasped life, i.e., the migīs´, to secure the mysterious power which he professes.

In addition to the practice of medical magic, the Jĕs´sakkīd´ sometimes resorts to a curious process to extract from the patient's body the malevolent beings or man´idōs which cause disease. The method of procedure is as follows: The Jĕs´sakkīd´ is provided with four or more tubular bones, consisting of the leg bones of large birds, each of the thickness of a finger and 4 or 5 inches in length. After the priest has fasted and chanted prayers for success, he gets down upon all fours close to the patient and with his mouth near the affected part. After using the rattle and singing most vociferously to cause the evil man´idō to take shelter at some particular spot, so that it may be detected and located by him, he suddenly touches that place with the end of one of the bones and immediately thereafter putting the other end into his mouth, as if it were a cigar, strikes it with the flat hand and sends it apparently down his throat. Then the second bone is treated in the same manner, as also the third and fourth, the last one being permitted to protrude from the mouth, when the end is put against the affected part and sucking is indulged in amid the most violent writhings and contortions in his endeavors to extract the man´idō. As this object is supposed to have been reached and swallowed by the Jĕs´sakkīd´ he crawls away to a short distance from the patient and relieves himself of the demon with violent 255 retchings and apparent suffering. He recovers in a short time, spits out the bones, and, after directing his patient what further medicine to swallow, receives his fee and departs. Further description of this practice will be referred to below and illustrated on Pl. XVIII.

The above manner of disposing of the hollow bones is a clever trick and not readily detected, and it is only by such acts of jugglery and other delusions that he maintains his influence and importance among the credulous.

figure described in text

Fig. 31. — Jĕs´sakkīd´ curing woman.

Fig. 32. —Jĕs´sakkīd´ curing man.

Fig. 31 represents a Jĕs´sakkīd´ curing a sick woman by sucking the demon through a bone tube. The pictograph was drawn upon a piece of birch bark which was carried in the owner's Midē´ sack, and was intended to record an event of importance.

No. 1 represents the actor, holding a rattle in hand. Around his head is an additional circle, denoting quantity (literally, more than an ordinary amount of knowledge), the short line projecting to the right indicating the tube used.

No. 2 is the woman operated upon.

Fig. 32 represents an exhibition by a Jĕs'sakkīd', a resident of White Earth, Minnesota. The priest is shown in No. 1 holding his rattle, the line extending from his eye to the patient's abdomen signifying that he has located the demon and is about to begin his exorcism. No. 2 is the patient lying before the operator.

FOURTH DEGREE.

midewigan as described in text

Fig. 33. —Diagram of Midē'wigân of the fourth degree.

The Midē'wigân, in which this degree is conferred, differs from the preceding structures by having open doorways in both the northern and southern walls, about midway between the eastern and western extremities and opposite to one another. Fig. 33 represents a ground plan, in which may also be observed the location of each of the four Midē' posts. Fig. 34 shows general view of same structure. A short distance from the eastern entrance is deposited the sacred stone, beyond which is an area reserved for the presents to be deposited by an applicant for initiation. The remaining two-thirds of the space toward the western door is occupied at regular intervals by four posts, the first being painted red with a band of green around the top. (Pl. XV , No. 1.) The second post is red, and has scattered over its surface spots of white clay to symbolize 256 the sacred mī'gis shell. Upon it is perched the stuffed skin of an owl—kŏ-kó-kŏ-ō'. (Pl. XV , No. 2.) The third post is black; but instead of being round is cut square. (Pl. XV , No. 3.) The fourth post, that nearest the western extremity, is in the shape of a cross, painted white, with red spots, excepting the lower half of the trunk, which is squared, the colors upon the four sides being white on the east, green on the south, red on the west, and black on the north. (Pl. XV , No. 4.)

view of midewigan

Fig. 34. —General view of Midē'wigân.

About 10 paces east of the main entrance, in a direct line between it and the sweat lodge, is planted a piece of thin board 3 feet high and 6 inches broad, the top of which is cut so as to present a three-lobed apex, as shown in Fig. 4 . The eastern side of this board is painted green; that facing the Midē'wigân red. Near the top is a small opening, through which the Midē' are enabled to peep into the interior of the sacred structure to observe the angry man'idōs occupying the structure and opposing the intrusion of anyone not of the fourth degree.

A cedar tree is planted at each of the outer corners of the Midē'wigân, and about 6 paces away from the northern, western, and southern entrances a small brush structure is erected, sufficiently large to admit the body. These structures are termed bears' nests, supposed to be points where the Bear Man'idō rested during the struggle he passed through while fighting with the malevolent man'idōs within to gain entrance and receive the fourth-degree initiation. Immediately within and to either side of the east and west entrances is planted a short post, 5 feet high and 8 inches thick, painted red upon the side facing the interior and black upon the reverse, at the base of each being laid a stone about as large as a human head. These four posts represent the four limbs and feet of the Bear Man'idō, who made the four entrances and forcibly entered and expelled the evil beings who had opposed him. The fourth-degree Midē' post— 257 the cross—furthermore symbolizes the four days' struggle at the four openings or doors in the north, south, east, and west walls of the structure.

PREPARATION OF CANDIDATE.

Under ordinary circumstances it requires at least one year before a Midē' of the third grade is considered eligible for promotion and it is seldom that a candidate can procure the necessary presents within that period, so that frequently a number of years elapse before any intimation by a candidate is made to the chief priest that the necessary requirements can be complied with. The chief reason of this delay is attributed to the fact that the fee to the officiating priests alone must equal in value and quantity four times the amount paid at the first initiation, and as the success in gathering the robes, skins, blankets, etc., depends upon the candidate's own exertions it will readily appear why so few ever attain the distinction sought. Should one be so fortunate, however, as to possess the required articles, he has only to make known the fact to the chief and assistant Midē' priests, when a meeting is held at the wig'iwam of one of the members and the merits of the candidate discussed. For this purpose tobacco is furnished by the candidate. The more valuable and more numerous the presents the more rapidly will his application be disposed of, and the more certainly will favorable consideration on it be had. It becomes necessary, as in former instances of preparation, for the candidate to procure the service of a renowned Midē', in order to acquire new or specially celebrated remedies or charms. The candidate may also give evidence of his own proficiency in magic without revealing the secrets of his success or the course pursued to attain it. The greater the mystery the higher he is held in esteem even by his jealous confrères.

There is not much to be gained by preparatory instruction for the fourth degree, the chief claims being a renewal of the ceremony of "shooting the mī'gis" into the body of the candidate, and enacting or dramatizing the traditional efforts of the Bear Man'idō in his endeavor to receive from the Otter the secrets of this grade. One who succeeds becomes correspondingly powerful in his profession and therefore more feared by the credulous. His sources of income are accordingly increased by the greater number of Indians who require his assistance. Hunters, warriors, and lovers have occasion to call upon him, and sometimes antidoting charms are sought, when the evil effects of an enemy's work are to be counteracted.

The instructor receives the visit of the candidate, and upon coming to a satisfactory agreement concerning the fee to be paid for the service he prepares his pupil by prompting him as to the part he is to enact during the initiation and the reasons therefor. The preparation and the merits of magic compounds are discussed, and 258 the pupil receives instruction in making effective charms, compounding love powder, etc. This love powder is held in high esteem, and its composition is held a profound secret, to be transmitted only when a great fee is paid. It consists of the following ingredients: Vermilion; powdered snakeroot (Polygala senega, L.); exiguam particulam sanguinis a puella effusi, quum in primis menstruis esset; and a piece of ginseng cut from the bifurcation of the root, and powdered. These are mixed and put into a small buckskin bag. The preparation is undertaken only after an offering to Ki'tshi Man'idō of tobacco and a Midē' song with rattle accompaniment. The manner of using this powder will be described under the caption of "descriptive notes. " It differs entirely from the powder employed in painting the face by one who wishes to attract or fascinate the object of his or her devotion. The latter is referred to by the Rev. Peter Jones[16] as follows:

There is a particular kind of charm which they use when they wish to obtain the object of their affections. It is made of roots and red ocher. With this they paint their faces, believing it to possess a power so irresistible as to cause the object of their desire to love them. But the moment this medicine is taken away and the charm withdrawn the person who before was almost frantic with love hates with a perfect hatred. It is necessary that the candidate take a sweat-bath once each day, for four successive days, at some time during the autumn months of the year preceding the year in which the initiation is to occur. This form of preparation is deemed agreeable to Ki'tshi Man'idō, whose favor is constantly invoked that the candidate may be favored with the powers supposed to be conferred in the last degree. As spring approaches the candidate makes occasional presents of tobacco to the chief priest and his assistants, and when the period of the annual ceremony approaches, they send out runners to members to solicit their presence, and, if of the fourth degree, their assistance.

INITIATION OF CANDIDATE.

The candidate removes to the vicinity of the Midē'wigân so as to be able to go through the ceremony of purgation four times before the day of initiation. The sudatory having been constructed on the usual site, east of the large structure, he enters it on the morning of the fifth day preceding the initiation and after taking a sweat-bath he is joined by the preceptor, when both proceed to the four entrances of the Midē'wigân and deposit at each a small offering of tobacco. This procedure is followed on the second and third days, also, but upon the fourth the presents are also carried along and deposited at the entrances, where they are received by assistants and suspended from the rafters of the interior. On the evening of the last day, the chief and officiating priests visit the candidate and his preceptor, 259 in the sweat-lodge, when ceremonial smoking is indulged in followed by the recitation of Midē' chants. The following (Pl. XVI, A) is a reproduction of the chant taught to and recited by the candidate. The original was obtained from an old mnemonic chart in use at Mille Lacs, Minnesota, in the year 1825, which in turn had been copied from a record in the possession of a Midē' priest at La Pointe, Wisconsin. Many of the words are of an older form than those in use at the present day. Each line may be repeated ad libitum.

mnemonic song
Plate XVI.a. Mnemonic Song.

line drawing Ni′-ka- ni-ka′- ni-ka′-
ni-na′, ni-na′, ni-na′,
I am the I am the I am the
Nika′ni, Nika′ni, Nika′ni,
man′-i-dō wig′-i-wam win′-di-ge′-un.
I am going into the sacred lodge.
[The speaker compares himself to the Bear Man′ido, and as such is represented at the entrance of the Midē′wigân.]

line drawing Ni′-ka- ni-ka′- ni-ka′-
ni-na′, ni-na′, ni-na′,
I am the I am the I am the
Nika′ni, Nika′ni, Nika′ni,
ni-kan′-gi-nun′-da wé-mĭ-dŭk′.
I "suppose" you hear me.
[The lines from the ear denotes hearing; the words are addressed to his auditors.]

line drawing Wâ′, he-wa′-ke- he-wa′-ke-
wa ke-wâ′, wâ′, wâ′.
He said, he said.
Signifies that Ki′tshi Man′idō, who is seen with the voice lines issuing from the mouth, and who promised the Ani′shinâ′bēg "life," that they might always live.

vertical lines Rest. A ceremonial smoke is now indulged in.

line drawing We′-ish ki-nun′-do-ni-ne′, ke-nosh′-ki-nun′-do-ni-ne′.
This is the first time you hear it.
[The lines of hearing are again shown; the words refer to the first time this is chanted as it is an intimation that the singer is to be advanced to the higher grade of the Midē′wiwin.]

line drawing Ha′we-na-ni-ka he-na′, he-nō′ mi-tē′-wi-wi′ gi′-ga-wa′-pi-no-dōn′.
You laugh, you laugh at the "grand medicine."
[The arms are directed towards Ki′tshi Man′idō, the creator of the sacred rite; the words refer to those who are ignorant of the Midē′wiwin and its teachings.]

line drawing Nu-wi′-ma-ne′, hē′, wi′-na-nun′-te-ma-ne′ ki′-pi-nan′.
I hear, but they hear it not.
[The speaker intimates that he realizes the importance of the Midē′ rite, but the uninitiated do not.]

260 Pe´-ne-sŭi´-a ke´-ke-kwi´-yan.
   I am sitting like a sparrow-hawk

line drawing

The singer is sitting upright, and is watchful, like a hawk watching for its prey. He is ready to observe, and to acquire, everything that may transpire in the Midē´ structure.

Upon the conclusion of the chant, the assembled Midē´ smoke and review the manner of procedure for the morrow's ceremony, and when these details have been settled they disperse, to return to their wig´iwams, or to visit Midē´ who may have come from distant settlements.

Early on the day of his initiation the candidate returns to the sudatory to await the coming of his preceptor. The gifts of tobacco are divided into parcels which may thus be easily distributed at the proper time, and as soon as the officiating priests have arrived, and seated themselves, the candidate produces some tobacco of which all present take a pipeful, when a ceremonial smoke-offering is made to Ki´tshi Man´idō. The candidate then takes his midē´ drum and sings a song of his own composition, or one which he may have purchased from his preceptor, or some Midē´ priest. The following is a reproduction of an old mnemonic song which the owner, Sikas´sigĕ, had received from his father who in turn had obtained it at La Pointe, Wisconsin, about the year 1800. The words are archaic to a great extent, and they furthermore differ from the modern language on account of the manner in which they are pronounced in chanting, which peculiarity has been faithfully followed below. The pictographic characters are reproduced in Pl. XVI, B. As usual, the several lines are sung ad libitum, repetition depending entirely upon the feelings of the singer.

mnemonic song
   Plate XVI.b. Mnemonic Song.
line drawing Hin´-to-nâ-ga-ne´ o-sa-ga-tshī´-gĕd o-do´-zhi-tōn´.
   The sun is coming up, that makes my dish.
   The dish signifies the feast to be made by the singer. The zigzag lines across the dish denote the sacred character of the feast. The upper lines are the arm holding the vessel.

line drawing Man´-i-dō i´-ya-nē´, ish´-ko-te´-wi-wa´-we-yan´.
   My spirit is on fire.
   The horizontal lines across the leg signify magic power of traversing space. The short lines below the foot denote flames, i. e., magic influence obtained by swiftness of communication with the man´idōs.

line drawing Ko´tshi-hâ-ya-nē´, nē´, ish´-ki-tŏ´-ya-ni, nin-do´-we-hē´, wi´-a-we-yan´.
   I want to try you, I am of fire.
   [The zigzag lines diverging from the mouth signify voice, singing; the apex upon the head superior knowledge, by means of which the singer wishes to try his Midē´ sack upon his hearer, to give evidence of the power of his influence.]

261 A pause. Ceremonial smoking is indulged in, after which the chant is continued.

vertical lines

line drawing Ni-mī´-ga-sim´-ma man´-i-dō, sa-ko´-tshi-na´.
   My mī´gis spirit, that is why I am stronger than you.
   The three spots denote the three times the singer has received the mī´gis by being shot; it is because this spirit is within him that he is more powerful than those upon the outside of the wigiwam who hear him.

line drawing Mī´-ga-ye´-nin en´-dy-ân, ya´, hŭ´, ya´, man´-i-dō´-ya.
   That is the way I feel, spirit.
   The speaker is filled with joy at his power, the mī´gis within him, shown by the spot upon the body, making him confident.

line drawing Yâ-gō´-sha-hī´, nâ´, ha´, ha´, Ya-gō´-sha-hi, man´-i-dō-wī´-yīn.
   I am stronger than you, spirit that you are.
   [He feels more powerful, from having received three times the mī´gis, than the evil spirit who antagonizes his progress in advancement.]

Upon the completion of this preliminary by the candidate, the priests emerge from the wig´iwam and fall in line according to their official status, when the candidate and preceptor gather up the parcels of tobacco and place themselves at the head of the column and start toward the eastern entrance of the Midē´wigân. As they approach the long post, or board, the candidate halts, when the priests continue to chant and drum upon the Midē´ drum. The chief Midē´ then advances to the board and peeps through the orifice near the top to view malevolent man´idōs occupying the interior, who are antagonistic to the entrance of a stranger. This spot is assumed to represent the resting place or "nest," from which the Bear Man´idō viewed the evil spirits during the time of his initiation by the Otter. The evil spirits within are crouching upon the floor, one behind the other and facing the east, the first being Mi-shi´-bi-shi´—the panther; the second, Me-shi´-kĕ—the turtle; the third, kwin´-go-â´-gī—the big wolverine; the fourth, wâ´-gŭsh—the fox; the fifth, ma-in´-gŭn—the wolf; and the sixth, ma-kwa´—the bear. They are the ones who endeavor to counteract or destroy the good wrought by the rites of the Midē´wiwin, and only by the aid of the good man´idōs can they be driven from the Midē´wigân so as to permit a candidate to enter and receive the benefits of the degree. The second Midē´ then views the group of malevolent beings, after which the third, and lastly the fourth priest looks through the orifice. They then advise 262 the presentation by the candidate of tobacco at that point to invoke the best efforts of the Midē´ Man´idōs in his behalf.

It is asserted that all of the malevolent man´idōs who occupied and surrounded the preceding degree structures have now assembled about this fourth degree of the Midē´wigân to make a final effort against the admission and advancement of the candidate: therefore he impersonates the good Bear Man´idō, and is obliged to follow a similar course in approaching from his present position the entrance of the structure. Upon hands and knees he slowly crawls toward the main entrance, when a wailing voice is heard in the east which sounds like the word hā´, prolonged in a monotone. This is ge´-gi-si´-bi-ga´-ne-dât man´idō. His bones are heard rattling as he approaches; he wields his bow and arrow; his long hair streaming in the air, and his body, covered with mī´gis shells from the salt sea, from which he has emerged to aid in the expulsion of the opposing spirits. This being the information given to the candidate he assumes and personates the character of the man´idō referred to, and being given a bow and four arrows, and under the guidance of his preceptor, he proceeds toward the main entrance of the structure while the officiating priests enter and station themselves within the door facing the west. The preceptor carries the remaining parcels of tobacco, and when the candidate arrives near the door he makes four movements with his bow and arrow toward the interior, as if shooting, the last time sending an arrow within, upon which the grinning spirits are forced to retreat toward the other end of the inclosure. The candidate then rushes in at the main entrance, and upon emerging at the south suddenly turns and again employs his bow and arrow four times toward the crowd of evil man´idōs, who have rushed toward him during the interval that he was within. At the last gesture of shooting into the inclosure, he sends forward an arrow, deposits a parcel of tobacco and crouches to rest at the so-called "bear's nest." During this period of repose the Midē´ priests continue to drum and sing. Then the candidate approaches the southern door again, on all fours, and the moment he arrives there he rises and is hurried through the inclosure to emerge at the west, where he turns suddenly, and imitating the manner of shooting arrows into the group of angry man´idōs within, he at the fourth movement lets fly an arrow and gets down into the western "bear's nest." After a short interval he again approaches the door, crawling forward on his hands and knees until he reaches the entrance, where he leaves a present of tobacco and is hastened through the inclosure to emerge at the northern door, where he again turns suddenly upon the angry spirits, and after making threatening movements toward them, at the fourth menace he sends an arrow among them. The spirits are now greatly annoyed by the magic power possessed by the candidate and the assistance rendered by the Midē´ Man´idōs, so that they are compelled to seek safety in flight. The candidate is resting in the northern "bear's nest," and as he again crawls toward the Midē´wigân, on hands and knees, he deposits another gift of a parcel of tobacco, then rises and is hurried through the interior to emerge at the entrance door, where he turns around, and seeing but a few angry man´idōs remaining, he takes his last arrow and aiming it at them makes four threatening gestures toward them, at the last sending the arrow into the structure, which puts to flight all opposition on the part of this host of man´idōs. The path is now clear, and after he deposits another gift of tobacco at the door he is led within, and the preceptor receives the bow and deposits it with the remaining tobacco upon the pile of blankets and robes that have by this time been removed from the rafters and laid upon the ground midway between the sacred Midē´ stone and the first Midē´ post.

The chief Midē´ priest then takes charge of the candidate, saying:

Mi´-a-shi´-gwa	wi-ka´-we-a´-kwa-mŭs-sin´-nŭk	Mī´-a-shi´-gwa
Now is the time	[to take] the path that has no end	Now is the time
wi-kan´-do-we-ân´	mi-ga-ī´-zhid wen´-	dzhi-bi-mâ´-dis.
I shall inform you [of]	that which I was told	the reason I live.

To this the second Midē´ priest remarks to the candidate, Wa´-shi-gân´-do-we-an´ mi-gai´-i-nŏk´ wa´-ka-no´-shi-dzin—which freely translated signifies: "The reason I now advise you is that you may heed him when he speaks to you." The candidate is then led around the interior of the inclosure, the assistant Midē´ fall in line of march and are followed by all the others present, excepting the musicians. During the circuit, which is performed slowly, the chief Midē´ drums upon the Midē´ drum and chants. The following, reproduced from the original, on Pl. XVII, B, consists of a number of archaic words, some of which are furthermore different from the spoken language on account of their being chanted, and meaningless syllables introduced to prolong certain accentuated notes. Each line and stanza may be repeated ad libitum.

mnemonic song

Plate XVII.b. Mnemonic Song.

line drawing Man´i-dō, hē´, nē´-yē´, man´-i-dō, hē´, nē´, yē´,
ēn´-da-na´-bi-yĕn wen´-dō-bi´-yĕn.

A spirit, a spirit, you who sit there, who sit there.

[The singer makes a spirit of the candidate by thus giving him new life, by again shooting into his body the sacred mīgis. The disk is the dish for feast of spirits in the dzhibai´ midē´wigân—"Ghost Lodge," the arms reaching towards it denoting the spirits who take food therefrom. The signification is that the candidate will be enabled to invoke and commune with the spirits of departed Midē´, and to learn of hidden powers.]

He´-ha-wa´-ni, yē´, he´-ha-wa´-ni, yē´,

line drawing nesh´-ga-na´-bi, hī´, hē´.

These words were chanted, while the following are those as spoken, apart from the music.

Â-wan´-ō-de´-no-wĭn nī´-bi-dĕsh´-ka-wĭn un´-de-no´-wĭn.

The fog wind goes from place to place whence the wind blows.

[The reason of the representation of a human form was not satisfactorily explained. The preceptor felt confident, however, that it signified a man′ĭdō who controls the fog, one different from one of the a-na′-mi-ki′, or Thunderers, who would be shown by the figure of an eagle, or a hawk, when it would also denote the thunder, and perhaps lightning, neither of which occurs in connection with the fog.]

vertical lines — Rest.

line drawing — Man′-i-dō′-we ni′-mi-nan′ ku-nĭg-ne man-to′-ke ni′-mi-ne′.

I who acknowledge you to be a spirit, and am dying.

The figure is an outline of the Midē′wigân with the sacred Midē′ stone indicated within, as also another spot to signify the place occupied by a sick person. The waving lines above and beneath the oblong square are magic lines, and indicate magic or supernatural power. The singer compares the candidate to a sick man who is seeking life by having shot into his body the mī′gis.

line drawing — Ga-kwe′-in-nân′ tshi-ha′-gĕ-nâ′-kwa′ ni-go′-tshi-ni′.

I am trying you who are the bear.

The Midē′ who is chanting is shown in the figure; his eyes are looking into the candidate's heart. The lines from the mouth are also shown as denoting speech, directed to his hearer. The horns are a representation of the manner of indicating superior powers.

line drawing — Pĭ-nē′-si ka′-ka-gī′-wai-yan′ wen′-dzhi man′-i-dō′wid.

The bird, the crow bird's skin is the reason why I am a spirit.

Although the crow is mentioned, the Thunder-bird (eagle) is delineated. The signification of the phrase is, that the speaker is equal in power to a man′ĭdō, at the time of using the Midē′ sack—which is of such a skin.

line drawing — A′shwin-gwe′-wi-he′-na nē′, ka′, tshi-wâ′-ba-ku-nēt′.

The sound of the Thunder is the white bear of fire.

The head is, in this instance, symbolical of the white bear man′ĭdō; the short lines below it denoting flame radiating from the body, the eyes also looking with penetrating gaze, as indicated by the double waving lines from each eye. The white bear man′ĭdō is one of the most powerful man′ĭdōs, and is so recognized.

By the time this chant is completed the head of the procession reaches the point of departure, just within the eastern door, and all of the members return to their seats, only the four officiating Midē′ remaining with the candidate and his preceptor. To search further 265 that no malevolent man′idōs may remain lurking within the Midē′wigân, the chief priests lead the candidate in a zigzag manner to the western door, and back again to the east. In this way the path leads past the side of the Midē′ stone, then right oblique to the north of the heap of presents, thence left oblique to the south of the first-degree post, then passing the second on the north, and so on until the last post is reached, around which the course continues, and back in a similar serpentine manner to the eastern door. The candidate is then led to the blankets, upon which he seats himself, the four officiating priests placing themselves before him, the preceptor standing back near the first of the four degree posts.

The Midē′ priest of the fourth rank or place in order of precedence approaches the kneeling candidate and in a manner similar to that which has already been described shoots into his breast the mī′gis; the third, second and first Midē′ follow in like manner, the last named alone shooting his mī′gis into the candidate's forehead, upon which he falls forward, spits out a mī′gis shell which he had previously secreted in his mouth, and upon the priests rubbing upon his back and limbs their Midē′ sacks he recovers and resumes his sitting posture.

The officiating priests retire to either side of the inclosure to find seats, when the newly received member arises and with the assistance of the preceptor distributes the remaining parcels of tobacco, and lastly the blankets, robes, and other gifts. He then begins at the southeastern angle of the inclosure to return thanks for admission, places both hands upon the first person, and as he moves them downward over his hair says: Mi-gwĕtsh′ ga-o′-shi-tō′-ĭn bi-mâ′-dĭ-sī-win—"Thanks, for giving to me life." The Midē′ addressed bows his head and responds, hau′, ē′,—yes when the newly admitted member steps back one pace, clasps his hands and inclines his head to the front. This movement is continued until all present have been thanked, after which he takes a seat in the southeastern corner of the inclosure.

A curious ceremony then takes place in which all the Midē′ on one side of the inclosure arise and approach those upon the other, each grasping his Midē′ sack and selecting a victim pretends to shoot into his body the mī′gis, whereupon the Midē′ so shot falls over, and after a brief attack of gagging and retching pretends to gain relief by spitting out of his mouth a mī′gis shell. This is held upon the left palm, and as the opposing party retreat to their seats, the side which has just been subjected to the attack moves rapidly around among one another as if dancing, but simply giving rapid utterance to the word hŏ′, hĕ′, hŏ′, hŏ′, hŏ′, hŏ′, and showing the mī′gis to everybody present, after which they place the flat hands quickly to the mouth and pretend again to swallow their respective shells. The members of this party then similarly attack their opponents, who 266 submit to similar treatment and go through like movements in exhibiting the mī′gis, which they again swallow. When quiet has been restored, and after a ceremonial smoke has been indulged in, the candidate sings, or chants, the production being either his own composition or that of some other person from whom it has been purchased. The chant presented herewith was obtained from Sĭkas′sigĕ, who had received it in turn from his father when the latter was chief priest of the Midē′wiwin at Mille Lacs, Minnesota. The pictographic characters are reproduced on Pl. XVII, A, and the musical notation, which is also presented, was obtained during the period of my preliminary instruction. The phraseology of the chant, of which each line and verse is repeated ad libitum as the singer may be inspired, is as follows:

mnemonic song
Plate XVII.a. Mnemonic Song.
line Drawing Na-wa-kwe′ in- do-nâ′-ga-nī′, do′-shi-tōn′, ga-nī′.
My At noon I make my dish, it, dish.
The singer refers to the feast which he gives to the Midē′ for admitting him into the Midē′wiwin.
musical notation
Do-na-ga-ni, Do-na-ga-ni, Do-na-ga-ni, Do-na-ga-ni,
Do-na-ga-ni, Do-na-ga-ni; Na-′kwa-wē′, In-do-shi-tōn Donagani,
Donaga-ni, Do-na-ga-ni, Do-na-ga-ni, Do-na-ga-ni, Do-na-ga-ni.
MIDI files: drum , flute , piano (default)
267
line Man′-ī-dō′ i-yan-nī′, Esh-ko′-te drawing nin-do-we′-yo-wĭn′,
ing I am such a spirit, My body is made of fire.
His power reaches to the sky, i.e., he has power to invoke the aid of Ki′tshi Man′idō. The four degrees which he has received are indicated by the four short lines at the tip of the hand.
musical notation
Ma′ni-dō-i-ya-ni, Ma′ni-dō-i-ya-ni, Ma′ni-dō-i-ya-ni,
Ma′ni-dō-i-ya-ni, Ma′ni-dō-i-ya-ni; Esh′ko-te nin-do we-yo-win, Manidōiya-ni, Ma′ni-dō-i-ya-ni,
Ma′ni-dō-i-ya-ni, Ma′ni-dō-i-ya-ni.
MIDI files: drum , flute , piano (default)
line Kō′tshihai′-o-nī′, drawing
Esh-ko′-te wa-ni′-yō.
I have tried it, My body is of fire.
He likens himself to the Bear Man′idō, and has like power by virtue of his mī′gis, which is shown below the lines running downward from the mouth. He is represented as standing in the Midē′wigân—where his feet rest.
musical notation
Ko′tshi-hai′o-ni, Ko′tshi-hai′o-ni, Ko′tshi-hai′o-ni,
Ko′tshihai′oni, Ko′tshi-hai′o-ni, Ko′tshi-hai′o-ni,
Ko′tshi-hai′o-ni, Ko′tshi-hai′o-ni, Esh′kote′wani′yo, Ko′tshihaioni.
Ko′tshihai′oni, Kotshihaioni, hĕ′ō, hĕ′ō.
MIDI files: drum , flute , piano (default)
vertical lines Pause. An offering of smoke is made to Ki′tshi Man′idō.
268 Ni-mī′-gi-sĭm′ man′-i-dō′-we, hwĕ′, hē′,
line drawing Sha-go-dzhĭ′-hi-na′.
My mī′gis spirit, I overpower death with.
[His body is covered with mī′gis as shown by the short lines radiating from the sides, and by this power he is enabled to overcome death.]
musical notation
Nimegasi mani dō-wē, hwē, hē, Nimegasi mani dō-wē, hwē, hē,
Shagodzhihinani-mega-si, Manido-wē, hwē, hē.
Ni-me-ga-si-ma-ni-dō-wē, hwē, hē.
MIDI files: drum , flute , piano (default)
line drawing Ni nin-man′-e-dō′-we-ya′.
Ya′-ho-ya′ man′-i-dō′-wa nin-da′-ho-ha′.
That is the way with me, spirit that I am.
[The hand shows how he casts the mī′gis forward into the person requiring life. He has fourfold power, i.e., he has received the mī′gis four times himself and is thus enabled to infuse into the person requiring it.]
musical notation
Ni′-ga-ne′ nin ma′ni-dō′we ya
Ni′-ga-ne′ nin ma′ni-dō′we ya,
Ya′ho-ya′ ma′nidō-we,
Nin′dohōha ni′gane, ma′ni-dō-we, ya, hē.
MIDI files: drum , flute , piano (default)
269 Ē-kotsh′-i-na′-ha,
Ē-kotsh′-ha man′-i-dō′ hwe-do′-line drawing
I hang it, I hang up the Spirit sack.
[After using his Midē′ sack he hangs it against the wall of the Midē′wigân, as is usually done during the ceremonial of initiation.]
musical notation
E-ko′tshi-na-ha, E-ko′tshi-na-ha, E-ko′tshi-na-ha,
E-ko′-tshi-na-ha, E-ko′-tshi-na-ha, E-ki′-tshi-ma′-ni-dō′ hwe-do-wi, E-ko′tshi-na-ha,
E-ko′tshi-na-ha, E-ko′tshi-na-ha, hĕ′a.
MIDI files: drum , flute , piano (default)
line drawing He-on′-dam-a′-ni, Man′-i-dō′ mi-de′-wi-he′ ne′-ma-da′-wi-dzig′.
Let them hear, Midē′ spirit, those who are sitting around.
[He invokes Ki′tshi Man′idō to make his auditors understand his power.]
musical notation
He-a-wi-non′-da-ma-ni hē, He-a-wi-nonda-ma-ni hē;
He′-a-wi-non-da-ma-ni hē, He′-a-wi-non-da-ma-ni hē;
Manidomidēwi hē, Nemadawi dzhig, Heawinondamani hē, hē, hē.
MIDI files: drum , flute , piano (default)
270
line He-a-we-na′ ni′-we-dō′,
drawing Man′-i-dō′ we-a-nī′
ing Nĭ′-ka-nā′ ni′-na-nā′.
He who is sleeping,
The Spirit, I bring him, a kinsman.
[In the employment of his powers he resorts to the help of Ki′tshi Man′idō—his kinsman or Midē′ colleague.]
musical notation
He-a-we-na-ne-we-dō, hō, He-a-we-na-ne-we-dō, hō,
He-a-we-na-ne-we-dō, hō, He-a-we-na-ne-we-dō, hō;
Ma′-ni-dō-we-a-ni ni-ka-na ni-ka-na, hō, hō.

MIDI files: drum , flute , piano (default)
line
drawing
ing
Man´-i-dō´ we-a-nī´
Ēsh-ke´-ta we´-a-nī´ man´-i-dō´ we´-a-nī´.

I am a spirit,
Fire is my spirit body.

[The hand reaches to the earth to grasp fire, showing his ability to do so without injury and illustrating in this manner his supernatural power.]

musical notation

Ma´ni-dō-wi-a-ni hē, Ma´ni-dō´wi-a-ni hē, Ma´-ni-dō´-wi-a-ni hē,
Ma´-ni-dō´-wi-a-ni hē, Ma´-ni-dō´wi-a-ni hē;
Esh´kato´weani hē, Ma´nidō´wiani hē, Ma´nidō´wia-ni hē.

MIDI files: drum , flute , piano (default)

271

line
drawing
ing
Ai-ya´-swa-kĭt-te´, hē´, he´,
Ha-ā´ se-wī´-kit-te´, hē´, hē´
Na-se´-ma-gŏt´ nin-dē´.

It is leaning,
My heart breathes.

[The phrase refers to the mī´gis within his heart. The short radiating lines indicate the magic power of the shell.]

musical notation

Hē´-a-si-wi-kit-te hē, Hē´-a-si-wi-kit-te hē, Hē´a-si-wikit-te hē,
Hē´-a-si-wi-kit-te hē, Na´simagot nin´de hē, Hē´-a-si-wi-kit-te hē,
Hē´-a-si-wi-kit-te hē´, Hē´-a-si-wi-kit-te hē´, Hē´a-si-wi-kitte hē.

MIDI files: drum , flute , piano (default)
Rest, or pause, after which dancing accompanies the remainder of the song.

lines
line
drawing
ing
Ni-ka´-nin-ko´-tshi´-ha ni´-ka-na Niwag-na-nin-ko´-tshi-ha.

Midē´ friends, I am trying, Midē´ friends, Midē´ friends, I am trying.

[His hand and arm crossed by lines to denote magic power, in reaching to grasp more than four degrees have given him; he has in view a fifth, or its equivalent.]

musical notation

Ni´-ka-ni ko´tshiha Ni´ka-ni ha,
Ni´-ka-ni ko´tshini Ni´-ka-ni ha,
Ni´-ka-ni ko´-tshi-ha Ni´-ka-ni ha.

MIDI files: drum , flute , piano (default)

272

line drawing
Ni drawing wa´ ni-be´-i-dōn´ ni-di´-na.

I hold that which I brought, and told him.

The singer is holding the mī´gis and refers to his having its power, which he desires Ki´tshi Man´idō to augment.

musical notation

He-ne-na-wa-ni-bei-dōn, He-ne-na-wa-ni-bei-dōn,
He-ne-na-wa-ni-bei-dōn, He-ne-na-wa-ni-bei-dōn.

MIDI files: drum , flute , piano (default)

line
drawing
ing
Ye´-we-ni´-mi-dē´, hwa´, da´, Ke-wa´-shi-mi-dē´, hĭ-a, hwē´,
Ye´-we-ni´-mi-dē?

Who is this grand Midē´? You have not much grand medicine.
Who is the Midē´?

[The first line, when used with the music, is a´-we-nin-o´-au-midē´. The whole phrase refers to boasters, who have not received the proper initiations which they profess. The figure is covered with mī´gis shells, as shown by the short lines attached to the body.]

musical notation

Ye-we-ni-mi-dē hwa, da. Ke-wa-shi-mi-dē hĭa, hwē,
Ye-we-ni-mi-dē hwa, da. Ke-wa-shi-mi-dē hĭa, hwe.
Ye-we-ni-mi-dē, Ye-we-ni-mi-dē hwa, da.

MIDI files: drum , flute , piano (default)

273

line drawing
Nai drawing yi na-ma´, ha´, Wa-na´-he-ne-ni-wa´, ha´,
O´-ta-be-we-ni´, mē´, hē´.

I can not reach it,
Only when I go round the Midē´wigân;
I can not reach it from where I sit.

[The mī´gis attached to the arrow signifies its swift and certain power and effect. The first line of the phrase, when spoken, is nin-na´-na-wi-nan´.]

musical notation

Nai-a-na-wi-na-ma ha, Na-a-na-wi-na-ma ha,
Nai-a-na-wi-na-ma ha, Na-a-na-wi-na-ma ha,
Wa-na-he-ne-ni-wa ha, O-ta-be-we-ni-me ha.

MIDI files: drum , flute , piano (default)

line
drawing
Ai-dai-wi na-wi´-na-ma´.

I can not strike him.

The speaker is weeping because he can not see immediate prospects for further advancement in the acquisition of power. The broken ring upon his breast is the place upon which he was shot with the mī´gis.

musical notation

Ai-ya-ha-na-wi-na-ma, Ai-ya-ha-na-w-na-ma,
Ai-ya-ha-na-wi-na-ma, Ai-ya-ha-na-w-na—ma, hĕŏ, hĕŏ, hĕŏ.

MIDI files: drum , flute , piano (default)

The following musical notation presents accurately the range of notes employed by the preceptor. The peculiarity of Midē´ songs lies in the fact that each person has his own individual series of notes which correspond to the number of syllables in the phrase and add thereto meaningless words to prolong the effect. When a song is taught, the words are the chief and most important part, the musical rendering of a second person may be so different from that of the person from whom he learns it as to be unrecognizable without 274   the words. Another fact which often presents itself is the absence of time and measure, which prevents any reduction to notation by full bars; e.g., one or two bars may appear to consist of four quarter notes or a sufficient number of quarters and eighths to complete such bars, but the succeeding one may consist of an additional quarter, or perhaps two, thus destroying all semblance of rythmic continuity. This peculiarity is not so common in dancing music, in which the instruments of percussion are employed to assist regularity and to accord with the steps made by the dancers, or vice versa.

In some of the songs presented in this

paper the bars have been omitted for the reasons presented above. The peculiarity of the songs as rendered by the preceptor is thus more plainly indicated.

When the chant is ended the ushers, who are appointed by the chief Midē´, leave the inclosure to bring in the vessels of food. This is furnished by the newly elected member and is prepared by his female relatives and friends. The kettles and dishes of food are borne around four times, so that each one present may have the opportunity of eating sufficiently. Smoking and conversation relating to the Midē´wiwin may then be continued until toward sunset, when, upon an intimation from the chief Midē´, the members quietly retire, leaving the structure by the western door. All personal property is removed, and upon the following day everybody departs.

DESCRIPTIVE NOTES.

The amount of influence wielded by Midē´ generally, and particularly such as have received four degrees, is beyond belief. The rite of the Midē´wiwin is deemed equivalent to a religion—as that term is commonly understood by intelligent people—and is believed to elevate such a Midē´ to the nearest possible approach to the reputed character of Mi´nabō´zho, and to place within his reach the supernatural power of invoking and communing with Ki´tshi Man´idō himself.

By reference to Pl. III, A, No. 98, it will be observed that the human figure is specially marked with very pronounced indications of mī´gis spots upon the head, the extremities, and more particularly the breast. These are placed where the mīgis was "shot" into the Midē´, and the functions of the several parts are therefore believed to be greatly augmented. All the spots are united by a line to denote unity and harmony of action in the exercise of power.

The mī´gis, typical of the fourth degree, consists of small pieces of deer horn, covered with red paint on one end and green upon the other. Sometimes but one color is employed for the entire object. The form is shown on Pl. XI, No. 6. No. 2, upon the same plate, represents a shell, used as a mī´gis, observed at White Earth.

Figs. 5-11, on Pl. XV, present several forms of painting midē´ 275 posts, as practiced by the several societies in Minnesota. Each society claims to preserve the ancient method. The cross, shown in No. 7, bears the typical colors—red and green—upon the upper half, while the lower post is square and colored white on the east, green on the south, red on the west, and black on the north. The Midē´ explain the signification of the colors as follows: White represents the east, the source of light and the direction from which the sacred mī´gis came; green, sha´manō the southern one, refers to the source of the rains, the direction from which the Thunderers come in the spring, they who revivify the earth; red refers to the land of the setting sun, the abode of the shadows or the dead; and north being black, because that is the direction from which come cold, hunger, and disease.

The words of the Midē´ priest alluding to "the path that has no end" refer to the future course and conduct of the candidate for the last degree, as well as to the possibility of attaining unlimited powers in magic, and is pictorially designated upon the chart on Pl. III, A, at No. 99. The path is devious and beset with temptations, but by strict adherence to the principles of the Midē´wiwin the Midē´ may reach the goal and become the superior of his confrères, designated Mi-ni´-si-nō´-shkwe, "he who lives on the island."

A Midē´-Wâběnō´ of this degree is dreaded on account of his extraordinary power of inflicting injury, causing misfortune, etc., and most remarkable tales are extant concerning his astounding performances with fire.

The following performance is said to have occurred at White Earth, Minnesota, in the presence of a large gathering of Indians and mixed bloods. Two small wig´iwams were erected, about 50 paces from each other, and after the Wâběnō´ had crawled into one of them his disparagers built around each of them a continuous heap of brush and firewood, which were then kindled. When the blaze was at its height all became hushed for a moment, and presently the Wâběnō´ called to the crowd that he had transferred himself to the other wig´iwam and immediately, to their profound astonishment, crawled forth unharmed.

This is but an example of the numerous and marvelous abilities with which the Wâběnō´ of the higher grade is accredited.

The special pretensions claimed by the Midē-Wâběnō´ have already been mentioned, but an account of the properties and manner of using the "love powder" may here be appropriate. This powder—the composition of which has been given—is generally used by the owner to accomplish results desired by the applicant. It is carried in a small bag made of buckskin or cloth, which the Wâběnō´ carefully deposits within his Midē´ sack, but which is transferred to another sack of like size and loaned to the applicant, for a valuable consideration.

276 During a recent visit to one of the reservations in Minnesota, I had occasion to confer with a Catholic missionary regarding some of the peculiar medical practices of the Indians, and the implements and other accessories employed in connection with their profession. He related the following incident as having but a short time previously come under his own personal observation:

One of the members of his church, a Norwegian, sixty-two years of age, and a widower, had for the last preceding year been considered by most of the residents as demented. The missionary himself had observed his erratic and frequently irrational conduct, and was impressed with the probable truth of the prevailing rumor. One morning, however, as the missionary was seated in his study, he was surprised to receive a very early call, and upon invitation his visitor took a seat and explained the object of his visit. He said that for the last year he had been so disturbed in his peace of mind that he now came to seek advice. He was fully aware of the common report respecting his conduct, but was utterly unable to control himself, and attributed the cause of his unfortunate condition to an occurrence of the year before. Upon waking one morning his thoughts were unwillingly concentrated upon an Indian woman with whom he had no personal acquaintance whatever, and, notwithstanding the absurdity of the impression, he was unable to cast it aside. After breakfast he was, by some inexplicable influence, compelled to call upon her, and to introduce himself, and although he expected to be able to avoid repeating the visit, he never had sufficient control over himself to resist lurking in the vicinity of her habitation.

Upon his return home after the first visit he discovered lying upon the floor under his bed, a Midē´ sack which contained some small parcels with which he was unfamiliar, but was afterward told that one of them consisted of "love powder." He stated that he had grown children, and the idea of marrying again was out of the question, not only on their account but because he was now too old. The missionary reasoned with him and suggested a course of procedure, the result of which had not been learned when the incident was related.

Jugglery of another kind, to which allusion has before been made, is also attributed to the highest class of Jĕs´sakkīd´. Several years ago the following account was related to Col. Garrick Mallery, U.S. Army, and myself, and as Col. Mallery subsequently read a paper before the Anthropological Society of Washington, District of Columbia, in which the account was mentioned, I quote his words:

Paul Beaulieu, an Ojibwa of mixed blood, present interpreter at White Earth Agency, Minnesota, gave me his experience with a Jĕs´sakkīd´, at Leech Lake, Minnesota, about the year 1858. The reports of his wonderful performances had reached the agency, and as Beaulieu had no faith in jugglers, he offered to wager 277 $100, a large sum, then and there, against goods of equal value, that the juggler could not perform satisfactorily one of the tricks of his repertoire to be selected by him (Beaulieu) in the presence of himself and a committee of his friends. The Jĕs´sakkân´—or Jĕs´sakkīd´ lodge—was then erected. The framework of vertical poles, inclined to the center, was filled in with interlaced twigs covered with blankets and birch-bark from the ground to the top, leaving an upper orifice of about a foot in diameter for the ingress and egress of spirits and the objects to be mentioned, but not large enough for the passage of a man's body. At one side of the lower wrapping a flap was left for the entrance of the Jĕs´sakkīd´.

A committee of twelve was selected to see that no communication was possible between the Jĕs´sakkīd´ and confederates. These were reliable people, one of them the Episcopal clergyman of the reservation. The spectators were several hundred in number, but they stood off, not being allowed to approach.

The Jĕs´sakkīd´ then removed his clothing, until nothing remained but the breech-cloth. Beaulieu took a rope (selected by himself for the purpose) and first tied and knotted one end about the juggler's ankles; his knees were then securely tied together, next the wrists, after which the arms were passed over the knees and a billet of wood passed through under the knees, thus securing and keeping the arms down motionless. The rope was then passed around the neck, again and again, each time tied and knotted, so as to bring the face down upon the knees. A flat river-stone, of black color—which was the Jĕs´sakkīd´'s ma´nidō or amulet—was left lying upon his thighs.

The Jĕs´sakkīd´ was then carried to the lodge and placed inside upon a mat on the ground, and the flap covering was restored so as to completely hide him from view.

Immediately loud, thumping noises were heard, and the framework began to sway from side to side with great violence; whereupon the clergyman remarked that this was the work of the Evil One and 'it was no place for him,' so he left and did not see the end. After a few minutes of violent movements and swayings of the lodge accompanied by loud inarticulate noises, the motions gradually ceased when the voice of the juggler was heard, telling Beaulieu to go to the house of a friend, near by, and get the rope. Now, Beaulieu, suspecting some joke was to be played upon him, directed the committee to be very careful not to permit any one to approach while he went for the rope, which he found at the place indicated, still tied exactly as he had placed it about the neck and extremities of the Jĕs´sakkīd´. He immediately returned, laid it down before the spectators, and requested of the Jĕs´sakkīd´ to be allowed to look at him, which was granted, but with the understanding that Beaulieu was not to touch him.

When the covering was pulled aside, the Jĕs´sakkīd´ sat within the lodge, contentedly smoking his pipe, with no other object in sight than the black stone minidō. Beaulieu paid his wager of $100.

An exhibition of similar pretended powers, also for a wager, was announced a short time after, at Yellow Medicine, Minnesota, to be given in the presence of a number of Army people, but at the threat of the Grand Medicine Man of the Leech Lake bands, who probably objected to interference with his lucrative monopoly, the event did not take place and bets were declared off.

Col. Mallery obtained further information, of a similar kind from various persons on the Bad River Reservation, and at Bayfield, Wisconsin. All of these he considered to be mere variants of a class of performances which were reported by the colonists of New England and the first French missionaries in Canada as early as 1613, where the general designation of "The Sorcerers" was applied to the whole body of Indians on the Ottawa River. These reports, it must be 278 remembered, however, applied only to the numerous tribes of the Algonkian linguistic family among which the alleged practices existed; though neighboring tribes of other linguistic groups were no doubt familiar with them, just as the Winnebago, Omaha and other allied tribes, profess to have "Medicine Societies," the secrets of which they claim to have obtained from tribes located east of their own habitat, that practiced the peculiar ceremony of "shooting small shells" (i.e., the mī′gis of the Ojibwa) into the candidate.

In Pl. XVIII is shown a Jĕs′sakkīd′ extracting sickness by sucking through bone tubes.

plate described in text
Plate XVIII. Jĕs′akkīd′ Removing Disease.

DZHIBAI′ MIDĒ′WIGÂN, OR "GHOST LODGE."

A structure erected by Indians for any purpose whatever, is now generally designated a lodge, in which sense the term is applied in connection with the word dzhibai′—ghost, or more appropriately shadow—in the above caption. This lodge is constructed in a form similar to that of the Midē′wigân, but its greatest diameter extends north and south instead of east and west. Further reference will be made to this in describing another method of conferring the initiation of the first degree of the Midē′wiwin. This distinction is attained by first becoming a member of the so-called "Ghost Society," in the manner and for the reason following:

After the birth of a male child it is customary to invite the friends of the family to a feast, designating at the same time a Midē′ to serve as godfather and to dedicate the child to some special pursuit in life. The Midē′ is governed in his decision by visions, and it thus sometimes happens that the child is dedicated to the "Grand Medicine," i.e., he is to be prepared to enter the society of the Midē′. In such a case the parents prepare him by procuring a good preceptor, and gather together robes, blankets, and other gifts to be presented at initiation.

Should this son die before the age of puberty, before which period it is not customary to admit any one into the society, the father paints his own face as before described, viz, red, with a green stripe diagonally across the face from left to right, as in Pl. VI , No. 4, or red with two short horizontal parallel bars in green upon the forehead as in Pl. VI , No. 5, and announces to the chief Midē′ priest his intention of becoming himself a member of the "Ghost Society" and his readiness to receive the first degree of the Midē′wiwin, as a substitute for his deceased son. Other members of the mourner's family blacken the face, as shown on Pl. VII , No. 5.

In due time a council of Midē′ priests is called, who visit the wig′iwam of the mourner, where they partake of a feast, and the subject of initiation is discussed. This wig′iwam is situated south and east 279 of the Midē′wigân, as shown in Fig. 35, which illustration is a reproduction of a drawing made by Sikas′sigĕ.

diagram as described in text
Fig. 35. —Indian diagram of ghost lodge.

The following is an explanation of the several characters:

No. 1 represents the wig′iwam of the mourner, which has been erected in the vicinity of the Midē′wigân, until after the ceremony of initiation.

No. 2 is the path supposed to be taken by the shadow (spirit) of the deceased; it leads westward to the Dzhibai′ Midē′wigân; literally, shadow-spirit wig′iwam.

No. 3, 4, 5, and 6, designate the places where the spirit plucks the fruits referred to—respectively the strawberry, the blueberry, the June cherries, and the plum.

No. 7 designates the form and location of the Dzhihai′ Midē′wigân. The central spot is the place of the dish of food for Dzhibai′ Man′idō—the good spirit—and the smaller spots around the interior of the inclosure are places for the deposit of dishes for the other Midē′ spirits who have left this earth.

No. 8 is the path which is taken by the candidate when going from his wig′iwam to the Midē′wigân.

No. 9 indicates the place of the sweat-lodge, resorted to at other periods of initiation.

No. 10 is the Midē′wigân in which the ceremony is conducted at the proper time.

It is stated that in former times the Ghost Lodge was erected west of the location of the mourner's wig′iwam, but for a long time this practice has been discontinued. The tradition relating to the Spirit's progress is communicated orally, while the dramatic representation is confined to placing the dishes of food in the Midē′wigân, which is selected as a fitting and appropriate substitute during the night preceding the initiation.

This custom, as it was practiced, consisted of carrying from the mourner's wig′iwam to the Ghost Lodge the dishes of food for the spirits of departed Midē′ to enjoy a feast, during the time that the Midē′ priests were partaking of one. A large dish was placed in the center of the structure by the mourner, from which the supreme Midē′ spirit was to eat. Dishes are now carried to the Midē′wigân, as stated above.

The chief officiating Midē′ then instructs the father of the deceased boy the manner in which he is to dress and proceed, as symbolizing the course pursued by the spirit of the son on the way to the spirit 280 world. The instructions are carried out, as far as possible, with the exception of going to an imaginary Ghost Lodge, as he proceeds only to the Midē′wigân and deposits the articles enumerated below. He is told to take one pair of bear-skin moccasins, one pair of wolf-skin, and one pair of birds' skins, in addition to those which he wears upon his feet; these are to be carried to the structure in which the Midē′ spirits are feasting, walking barefooted, picking a strawberry from a plant on the right of the path and a blueberry from a bush on the left, plucking June cherries from a tree on the right and plums on the left. He is then to hasten toward the Ghost Lodge, which is covered with mī′gis, and to deposit the fruit and the moccasins; these will be used by his son's spirit in traveling the road of the dead after the spirits have completed their feast and reception of him. While the candidate is on his mission to the Ghost Lodge (for the time being represented by the Midē′wigân) the assemblage in the wig′iwam chant the following for the mourner: Yan′-i-ma-tsha′, yan′-i-ma-tsha′, ha′, yan′-i-ma-tsha´ yan´-i-ma-tsha´ ha´, yu´-te-no-win´ gē´, hē´ nin-de´-so-ne´—"I am going away, I am going away, I am going away, to the village I walk"—i.e., the village of the dead.

The person who desires to receive initiation into the Midē´wigân, under such circumstances, impersonates Minabō´zho, as he is believed to have penetrated the country of the abode of shadows, or ne´-ba-gī´-zis—"land of the sleeping sun." He, it is said, did this to destroy the "Ghost Gambler" and to liberate the many victims who had fallen into his power. To be enabled to traverse this dark and dismal path, he borrowed of Kŏ-ko´-kŏ-ō´—the owl—his eyes, and received also the services of wē´-we-tē´-si-wŭg—the firefly, both of which were sent back to the earth upon the completion of his journey. By referring to Pl. III , A , the reference to this myth will be observed as pictorially represented in Nos. 110 to 114. No. 110 is the Midē´wigân from which the traveler has to visit the Dzhibai´ Midē´wigân (No. 112) in the west. No. 113, represented as Kŏ-ko´-kŏ-ō´—the owl—whose eyes enabled Mī´nabō´zho to follow the path of the dead (No. 114); the owl skin Midē´ sack is also sometimes used by Midē´ priests who have received their first degree in this wise. The V-shaped characters within the circle at No. 111 denote the presence of spirits at the Ghost Lodge, to which reference has been made.

The presents which had been gathered as a gift or fee for the deceased are now produced and placed in order for transportation to the Midē´wigân, early on the following morning.

The Midē´ priests then depart, but on the next morning several of them make their appearance to assist in clearing the Midē´wigân of the dishes which had been left there over night, and to carry thither the robes, blankets, and other presents, and suspend them from the rafters. Upon their return to the candidate's wig´iwam, the Midē´ priests gather, and after the candidate starts to lead the procession 281 toward the Midē´wigân, the priests fall in in single file, and all move forward, the Midē´ priests chanting the following words repeatedly, viz: Ki-e´-ne-kwo-tâ´ ki-e´-ne-kwo-tâ´, ha´, ha´, ha´, nōs e´wi-e´, hē´, ki´-na-ka´-ta-mŭn´ do-nâ´-gan—"I also, I also, my father, leave you my dish."

This is sung for the deceased, who is supposed to bequeath to his father his dish, or other articles the names of which are sometimes added.

The procession continues toward and into the Midē´wigân, passing around the interior by the left side toward the west, north, and east to a point opposite the space usually reserved for the deposit of goods, where the candidate turns to the right and stands in the middle of the inclosure, where he now faces the Midē´ post in the west. The members who had not joined the procession, but who had been awaiting its arrival, now resume their seats, and those who accompanied the candidate also locate themselves as they desire, when the officiating priests begin the ceremony as described in connection with the initiation for the first degree after the candidate has been turned over to the chief by the preceptor.

Sometimes the mother of one who had been so dedicated to the Midē´wiwin is taken into that society, particularly when the father is absent or dead.

INITIATION BY SUBSTITUTION.

It sometimes happens that a sick person can not be successfully treated by the Midē´, especially in the wig´iwam of the patient, when it becomes necessary for the latter to be carried to the Midē´wigân and the services of the society to be held. This course is particularly followed when the sick person or the family can furnish a fee equivalent to the gift required for initiation under ordinary circumstances.

It is believed, under such conditions, that the evil man´idōs can be expelled from the body only in the sacred structure, at which place alone the presence of Ki´tshi Man´idō may be felt, after invocation, and in return for his aid in prolonging the life of the patient the latter promises his future existence to be devoted to the practice and teachings of the Midē´wiwin. Before proceeding further, however, it is necessary to describe the method pursued by the Midē´ priest.

The first administrations may consist of mashki´kiwabū´, or medicine broth, this being the prescription of the Midē´ in the capacity of mashki´kike´winī´nī, or herbalist, during which medication he resorts to incantation and exorcism, accompanying his song by liberal use of the rattle. As an illustration of the songs used at this period of the illness, the following is presented, the mnemonic characters being reproduced on Pl. XVI , C . The singing is monotonous and doleful, though at times it becomes animated and discordant.

282

mnemonic song

Plate XVI.c. Mnemonic Song.

he´-dowia-gât in-da´-kwo-nan
That which I live upon has been put on this dish by the spirit.

Ki´tshi Man´idō provides the speaker with the necessary food for the maintenance of life. The dish, or feast, is shown by the concentric rings, the spirit's arm is just below it.

Mo-I-ki-yan tshik´-ko-min´.
living I bring life to the people.

The speaker, as the impersonator of the sacred Otter, brings life. The Otter is just emerging from the surface of the water, as he emerged from the great salt sea before the Âni´shi-nâ´beg, after having been instructed by Mi´nabō´zho to carry life to them.

Ni´-no-mūn´ mash-ki´-ki
drawI can also take medicine from the in lodge, or the earth

The Midē´'s arm is reaching down to extract magic remedies from the earth. The four spots indicate the remedies, while the square figure denotes a hole in the ground.

Rest. During this interval the Midē´'s thoughts dwell upon the sacred character of the work in which he is engaged.

Ni´-nin-dē´ in´-dai-yo´.
crawlIt is all in my heart, the life.
ing The concentric circles indicates the mī´gis, life, within the heart, the former showing radiating lines to

denote its magic power.

line drawing
Mī'shōmĭse-an-kĭnk´.
The spirit saw me and sent me medicine from above.
The figure is that of Kī'tshi Man´idō, who granted power to the speaker.

line drawing
Ōn´-de-na mi-tĭz´-kŭnk.
I also on the trees, that from which I take life.
The tree bears "medicine" which the speaker has at his command, and is enabled to use.

283 When the ordinary course of treatment fails to relieve the patient the fact is made known to the Midē´ priests and he is consequently taken to the Midē´wigân and laid upon blankets so that part of his body may rest against the sacred midē´ stone. Associate Midē´ then attend, in consultation, with the Midē´-in-chief, the other members present occupying seats around the walls of the structure.

The accompanying lecture is then addressed to the sick person, viz:
Mi-shosh´-yâ-gwa ga´-a-nin-nan´ gi´-de-wēn´-du-nŭn ne´-tun-ga´-da-da-we´-in man´-i-dōmī´-gis. Kit´-ti-mâ´-gī-si ē´-ni-dau´-â-ya-we´-yĭn o-ma´-e-nâ´-sa-ba-bĭt bī-ī-sha´-gaban´-dē-a gi-bī´-sha-ban-da´-ĕt na-pĭsh-kâ-tshi-dōsh ke´-a-yū-ĭn-ki-go gŏt-tâ-sō-nĕn´, mi-a-shi´-gwa-gō-dĭn´-na-wât dzhi-ma´-di-a-kad´-dō-yōn bi-mâ-di-si-wĭn´.

The following is a free translation of the above:
The time of which I spoke to you has now arrived, and you may deem it necessary to first borrow the sacred mī´gis. Who are you that comes here as a supplicant? Sit down opposite to me, where I can see you and speak to you, and fix your attention upon me, while you receive life you must not permit your thoughts to dwell upon your present condition, but to support yourself against falling into despondency. Now we are ready to try him; now we are ready to initiate him.

The reference to borrowing a mī´gis signifies that the patient may have this mysterious power "shot into his body" where he lies upon the ground and before he has arrived at the place where candidates are properly initiated; this, because of his inability to walk round the inclosure.

The last sentence is spoken to the assisting Midē´. The following song is sung, the mnemonic characters pertaining thereto being reproduced on Pl. XVI, D.

mnemonic song
Plate XVI.d. Mnemonic Song.

line drawing
O-da´-pi-nŭng´-mung oâ´-ki-wen´-dzhi man´-i-dō we´-an-ī-win´-zhi-gu-sân´.
We are going to take the sacred medicine out of the ground.
[The speaker refers to himself and the assistants as resorting to remedies adopted after consultation, the efficiency thereof depending upon their combined prayers. The arm is represented as reaching for a remedy which is surrounded by lines denoting soil.]

line drawing
We-a´-ki man´-i-dō we-an-gīs´.
The ground is why I am a spirit, my son.
The lower horizontal line is the earth, while the magic power which he possesses is designated by short vertical wavy lines which reach his body.

vertical lines
Rest.

line drawing
Nish´-u-we-ni-mi´-qu nish´-u-ng-ni-mi´-qu we´-gi ma´-ŏ-dzhig´.
The spirits have pity; the spirits have pity on me.
The Midē´ is supplicating the Midē´ spirits for aid in his wishes to cure the sick.

284 Kish´-u-we-ni-mi´-qu ki´-shi´-gŭng don´-dzhi-wa´-wa-mĭk.
line drawing
The spirits have pity on me; from on high I see you.
The sky is shown by the upper curved lines, beneath which the Midē´ is raising his arm in supplication.

line drawing
Man´-i-dō´-â ni´-o.
My body is a spirit.
The Midē´ likens himself to the Bear Man´idō, the magic powers of which are shown by the lines across the body and short strokes upon the back.

line drawing
Pi-ne´-si-wi-ân´ ke-ke´-u-wi-an´.
A little bird I am: I am the hawk.
Like the thunderer, he penetrates the sky in search of power and influence.

line drawing
Man´-i-dō´ nu´-tu wa´-kan.
Let us hear the spirit.
The Ki´tshi Man´idō is believed to make known his presence, and all are enjoined to listen for such intimation.

line drawing
Kau´-nun-ta´-wa man´-i-dō´ wi´-da-ku-ē´, hē´, ki´-a-ha-mī´.
You might hear that he is a spirit.
The line on the top of the head signifies the person to be a superior being.

line drawing
Ka´-ke-na gus-sâ´ o´-mi-si´-nī´-na´-ēn.
I am afraid of all, that is why I am in trouble.
The Midē´ fears that life can not be prolonged because the evil man´idōs do not appear to leave the body of the sick person. The arm is shown reaching for mī´gis, or life, the strength of the speaker's, having himself received it four times, does not appear to be of any avail.

Should the patient continue to show decided symptoms of increased illness, the singing or the use of the rattle is continued until life is extinct, and no other ceremony is attempted; but if he is no worse after the preliminary course of treatment, or shows any improvement, the first attendant Midē´ changes his songs to those of a more boastful character. The first of these is as follows, chanted repeatedly and in a monotonous manner, viz:

A´-si-na´-bi-hu´-ya,   a-si´-na´-b-hu´-ya.
I have changed   I have changed

my looks, my looks.

[This refers to the appearance of the Midē′ stone which it is believed absorbs some of the disease and assumes a change of color.]

Nish′-a-we′nī′, hū′, gū′, mi-dē′, wug, a-ne′-ma-bī′-tshig.

The Midē′ have pity on me, those who are sitting around, and those who are sitting from us.

[The last line refers to those Midē′ who are sitting, though absent from the Midē′wigân.]

285   The following illustrates the musical rendering:

musical notation

A-si-na-bi-hŭ-i-ya, A-si-na-bi-hŭ-i-ya, A-si-na-bi-hŭ-i-ya hĭa,
A-si-na-bi-hŭ-i-ya, A-si-na-bi-hŭ-i-ya hĭa.

MIDI files: drum , flute , piano (default)

musical notation

Nish-a-wi-in-hu gū, O-ko-mi-dē-wog hē, A-ne-ma-bi-tshig hē,
Nishawiinhu gū, O-ko-mi-dē-wog hē,
Nish-a-wi-ni-hu gū O-ko-mi-dē-wog hē.

MIDI files: drum , flute , piano (default)

As the patient continues to improve the song of the Midē′ becomes more expressive of his confidence in his own abilities and importance.

The following is an example in illustration, viz:

Ni-ne′-ta-we-hē′ wa-wâ′-bâ-ma′ man′-i-dō, wa-wâ′-bâ-ma′.

[I am the only one who sees the spirit, who sees the spirit.]

Nin′-da-nī′-wĭ-a, nin′-da-nī′-wĭ-a.

I surpass him,   I surpass him.

[The speaker overcomes the malevolent man′idō and causes him to take flight.]

Na′-sa-ni-nēn′-di-ya   a-we′-si-yŏk′ no-gwe′-no′-wōk.

See how I act, beasts I shoot on the wing.

[The signification of this is, that he "shoots at them as they fly," referring to the man′idōs as they escape from the body.]

The following is the musical notation of the above, viz:

musical notation

Ni-ne-ta-we-hē wa-wâ′bâ-ma man-i-dō wa-wâ′-bâ-ma man-i-dō,
Ni-ne-ta-we-hē wa-wâ′-bâ-ma man-i-dō, wa-wâ′-bâ-ma man-i-dō.

MIDI files: drum , flute , piano (default)

286

musical notation

Hen-ta-ne-we-a, Hen-ta-ne-we-a, Hen-ta-ne-we-a, Hen-ta-ne-we-a,
Hen-ta-ne-we-a, Hen-ta-ne-we-a, Hen-ta-ne-we-a, Hen-ta-ne-we-a,
Hen-ta-ne-we-a, Hen-ta-ne-we-a, Hen-ta-ne-we-a, hō.

MIDI files: drum , flute , piano (default)

musical notation

Na-sa-ni-nen-di-ya, Na-sa-ni-nen-di-ya, Na-sa-ni-nen-di-ya,
Awasiyōk, Nogwenowōk.

MIDI files: drum , flute , piano (default)

If the patient becomes strong enough to walk round the inclosure he is led to the western end and seated upon a blanket, where he is initiated. If not, the mī′gis is "shot into his body" as he reclines against the sacred stone, after which a substitute is selected from among the Midē′ present, who takes his place and goes through the remainder of the initiation for him. Before proceeding upon either course, however, the chief attendant Midē′ announces his readiness in the following manner: Mī′-o-shi′-gwa, wi-kwod′-gi-o-wŏg′ ga-mâ′-dzhi-a-ka′-dŭng bi-mâ-di-si-wĭn′—"Now we are ready to escape from this and to begin to watch life." This signifies his desire to escape from his present procedure and to advance to another course of action, to the exercise of the power of giving life by transferring the sacred mī′gis.

The remainder of the ceremony is then conducted as in the manner described as pertains to the first degree of the Midē′wiwin.

SUPPLEMENTARY NOTES.

PICTOGRAPHY.

Before concluding, it may be of interest to refer in some detail to several subjects mentioned in the preceding pages. The mnemonic songs are in nearly every instance incised upon birch bark by means of a sharp-pointed piece of bone or a nail. The inner surface of the bark is generally selected because it is softer than the reverse. Bark for such purposes is peeled from the trunk during the spring months. On the right hand upper corner of Pl. XIX is reproduced a portion 287 of a mnemonic song showing characters as thus drawn. The specimen was obtained at White Earth, and the entire song is presented on Pl. XVI , C . A piece of bark obtained at Red Lake, and known to have been incised more than seventy years ago, is shown on the right lower corner of Pl. XIX . The drawings are upon the outer surface and are remarkably deep and distinct. The left hand specimen is from the last named locality, and of the same period, and presents pictographs drawn upon the inner surface.

plate described in text
Plate XIX. Sacred Birch Bark Records.

In a majority of songs the characters are drawn so as to be read from left to right, in some from right to left, and occasionally one is found to combine both styles, being truly boustrophic. Specimens have been obtained upon which the characters were drawn around and near the margin of an oblong piece of bark, thus appearing in the form of an irregular circle.

The pictographic delineation of ideas is found to exist chiefly among the shamans, hunters, and travelers of the Ojibwa, and there does not appear to be a recognized system by which the work of any one person is fully intelligible to another. A record may be recognized as pertaining to the Midē′ ceremonies, as a song used when hunting plants, etc.; but it would be impossible for one totally unfamiliar with the record to state positively whether the initial character was at the left or the right hand. The figures are more than simply mnemonic; they are ideographic, and frequently possess additional interest from the fact that several ideas are expressed in combination. Col. Garrick Mallery, U.S. Army, in a paper entitled "Recently

Discovered Algonkian Pictographs," read before the American Association for the Advancement of Science, at Cleveland, 1888, expressed this fact in the following words:

It is desirable to explain the mode of using the Midē´ and other bark records of the Ojibwa and also those of other Algonkian tribes to be mentioned in this paper. The comparison made by Dr. E. B. Tylor of the pictorial alphabet to teach children "A was an archer," etc. , is not strictly appropriate in this case. The devices are not only mnemonic, but are also ideographic and descriptive. They are not merely invented to express or memorize the subject, but are evolved therefrom. To persons acquainted with secret societies a good comparison for the charts or rolls would be what is called the tressel board of the Masonic order, which is printed and published and publicly exposed without exhibiting any of the secrets of the order, yet is not only significant, but useful to the esoteric in assistance to their memory as to degrees and details of ceremony.

A more general mode of explaining the so-called symbolism is by a suggestion that the charts of the order or the song of a myth should be likened to the popular illustrated poems and songs lately published in Harper's Magazine for instance, "Sally in our Alley," where every stanza has an appropriate illustration. Now, suppose that the text was obliterated forever, indeed the art of reading lost, the illustrations remaining, as also the memory to many persons of the ballad. The illustrations kept in order would supply always the order of the stanzas and also the general subject-matter of each particular stanza and the latter would be a reminder of the words. This is what the rolls of birch bark do to the initiated Ojibwa, and what Schoolcraft pretended in some cases to show, but what for actual 288 understanding requires that all the vocables of the actual songs and charges of the initiation should be recorded and translated. This involves not only profound linguistic study, but the revelation of all the mysteries. In other instances the literation in the aboriginal language of the nonesoteric songs and stories and their translation is necessary to comprehend the devices by which they are memorized rather than symbolized. Nevertheless, long usage has induced some degree of ideography and symbolism.

plate described in text
Plate XX. Sacred Bark Scroll And Contents.

On Pl. XX are presented illustrations of several articles found in a Midē´ sack which had been delivered to the Catholic priest at Red Lake over seventy years ago, when the owner professed Christianity and forever renounced (at least verbally) his pagan profession. The information given below was obtained from Midē´ priests at the above locality. They are possessed of like articles, being members of the same society to which the late owners of the relics belonged. The first is a birch-bark roll, the ends of which were slit into short strips, so as to curl in toward the middle to prevent the escaping of the contents. The upper figure is that of the Thunder god, with waving lines extending forward from the eyes, denoting the power of peering into futurity. This character has suggested to several Midē´ priests that the owner might have been a Midē´-Jĕs´sakkĭd´. This belief is supported by the actual practice pursued by this class of priests when marking their personal effects. The lower figure is that of a buffalo, as is apparent from the presence of the hump. Curiously enough both eyes are drawn upon one side of the head, a practice not often followed by Indian artists.

The upper of the four small figures is a small package, folded, consisting of the inner sheet of birch-bark and resembling paper both in consistence and color. Upon the upper fold is the outline of the Thunder bird. The next two objects represent small boxes made of pine wood, painted or stained red and black. They were empty when received, but were no doubt used to hold sacred objects. The lowest figure of the four consists of a bundle of three small bags of cotton wrapped with a strip of blue cloth. The bags contain, respectively, love powder, hunter's medicine—in this instance red ocher and powdered arbor vitæ leaves—and another powder of a brownish color, with which is mixed a small quantity of ground medicinal plants.

relics as described in text
Plate XXI. Midē´ Relics From Leech Lake.

The roll of birch-bark containing these relics inclosed also the skin of a small rodent (Spermophilus sp.?) but in a torn and moth-eaten condition. This was used by the owner for purposes unknown to those who were consulted upon the subject. It is frequently, if not generally, impossible to ascertain the use of most of the fetiches and other sacred objects contained in Midē´ sacks of unknown ownership, as each priest adopts his own line of practice, based upon a variety of reasons, chiefly the nature of his fasting dreams.

Fancy sometimes leads an individual to prepare medicine sticks that are of curious shape or bear designs of odd form copied after 289 something of European origin, as exemplified in the specimen illustrated on. Pl. XXI , Nos. 1 and 2, showing both the obverse and reverse. The specimen is made of ash wood and measures about ten inches in length. On the obverse side, besides the figures of man´-idōs, such as the Thunder bird, the serpent, and the tortoise, there is the outline of the sun, spots copied from playing cards, etc.; upon the reverse appear two spread hands, a bird, and a building, from the top of which floats the American flag. This specimen was found among the effects of a Midē´ who died at Leech Lake, Minnesota, a few years ago, together with effigies and other relics already mentioned in another part of this paper.

MUSIC.

In addition to the examples of Indian music that have been given, especially the songs of shamans, it may be of interest to add a few remarks concerning the several varieties of songs or chants. Songs employed as an accompaniment to dances are known to almost all the members of the tribe, so that their rendition is nearly always the same. Such songs are not used in connection with mnemonic characters, as there are, in most instances, no words or phrases recited, but simply a continued repetition of meaningless words or syllables. The notes are thus rhythmically accentuated, often accompanied by beats upon the drum and the steps of the dancers.

An example of another variety of songs, or rather chants, is presented in connection with the reception of the candidate by the Midē´ priest upon his entrance into the Midē´wigân of the first degree. In this instance words are chanted, but the musical rendition differs with the individual, each Midē´ chanting notes of his own, according to his choice or musical ability. There is no set formula, and such songs, even if taught to others, are soon distorted by being sung according to the taste or ability of the singer. The musical rendering of the words and phrases relating to the signification of mnemonic characters depends upon the ability and inspired condition of the singer; and as each Midē´ priest usually invents and prepares his own songs, whether for ceremonial purposes, medicine hunting, exorcism, or any other use, he may frequently be unable to sing them twice in exactly the same manner. Love songs and war songs, being of general use, are always sung in the same style of notation.

The emotions are fully expressed in the musical rendering of the several classes of songs, which are, with few exceptions, in a minor key. Dancing and war songs are always in quick time, the latter frequently becoming extraordinarily animated and boisterous as the participants become more and more excited.

Midē´ and other like songs are always more or less monotonous, though they are sometimes rather impressive, especially if delivered 290 by one sufficiently emotional and possessed of a good voice. Some of the Midē´ priests employ few notes, not exceeding a range of five, for all songs, while others frequently cover the octave, terminating with a final note lower still.

The statement has been made that one Midē´ is unable either to recite or sing the proper phrase pertaining to the mnemonic characters of a song belonging to another Midē´ unless specially instructed. The representation of an object may refer to a variety of ideas of a similar, though not identical, character. The picture of a bear may signify the Bear man´idō as one of the guardians of the society; it may pertain to the fact that the singer impersonates that man´idō; exorcism of the malevolent bear spirit may be thus claimed; or it may relate to the desired capture of the animal, as when drawn to insure success for the hunter. An Indian is slow to acquire the exact phraseology, which is always sung or chanted, of mnemonic songs recited to him by a Midē´ preceptor.

An exact reproduction is implicitly believed to be necessary, as otherwise the value of the formula would be impaired, or perhaps even totally destroyed. It frequently happens, therefore, that although an Indian candidate for admission into the Mīdē´wiwin may already have prepared songs in imitation of those from which he was instructed, he may either as yet be unable to sing perfectly the phrases relating thereto, or decline to do so because of a want of confidence. Under such circumstances the interpretation of a record is far from satisfactory, each character being explained simply objectively, the true import being intentionally or unavoidably omitted. An Ojibwa named "Little Frenchman," living at Red Lake, had received almost continuous instruction for three or four years, and although he was a willing and valuable assistant in other matters pertaining to the subject under consideration, he was not sufficiently familiar with some of his preceptor's songs to fully explain them. A few examples of such mnemonic songs are presented in illustration, and for comparison with such as have already been recorded. In each instance the Indian's interpretation of the character is given first, the notes in brackets being supplied in further explanation. Pl. XXII , A , is reproduced from a birch-bark song; the incised lines are sharp and clear, while the drawing in general is of a superior character. The record is drawn so as to be read from right to left.

mnemonic song
Plate XXII.a. Mnemonic Song.
line From whence I sit.
drawing [The singer is seated, as the lines indicate contact with the surface beneath, though the latter is not shown. The short line extending from the mouth indicates voice, and probably signifies, in this instance, singing.]
291 The big tree in the center of the earth.
line
draw- [It is not known whether or not this relates to the first destruction of the earth, when
ing Mi´nabō´zho escaped by climbing a tree which continued to grow and to protrude above the surface of the flood. One Midē´ thought it related to a particular medicinal tree which was held in estimation beyond all others, and thus represented as the chief of the earth.]
line I will float down the fast running
draw- stream.
ing [Strangely enough, progress by water is here designated by footprints instead of using the outline of a canoe. The etymology of the Ojibwa word used in this connection may suggest footprints, as in the Delaware language one word for river signifies "water road," when in accordance therewith "footprints" would be in perfect harmony with the general idea.]
line d The place that is feared I inhabit,
ing the swift-running stream I inhabit.
[The circular line above the Midē´ denotes obscurity, i.e., he is hidden from view and represents himself as powerful and terrible to his enemies as the water monster.]
line You who speak to me.
drawing

line I have long horns.
drawing [The Midē' likens himself to the water monster, one of the malevolent serpent man'idōs who antagonize all good, as beliefs and practices of the Midē'wiwin.]

vertical lines A rest or pause.

line I, seeing, follow your example.
drawing

line You see my body, you see my body, you see my nails are worn off in grasping the stone.
drawing [The Bear man'idō is represented as the type now assumed by the Midē'. He has a stone within his grasp, from which magic remedies are extracted.]

292 You, to whom I am speaking.
line [A powerful Man'idō', the panther, is in an inclosure and to him the Midē' addresses his request.]
drawing

line I am swimming—floating—down smoothly.
drawing [The two pairs of serpentine lines indicate the river banks, while the character between them is the Otter, here personated by the Midē'.]

vertical lines Bars denoting a pause.

line I have finished my drum.
drawing [The Midē' is shown holding a Midē' drum which he is making for use in a ceremony.]

line My body is like unto you.
drawing [The mī'gis shell, the symbol of purity and the Midē'wiwin.]

line Hear me, you who are talking to me!
drawing [The speaker extends his arms to the right and left indicating persons who are talking to him from their respective places. The lines denoting speech—or hearing—pass through the speaker's head to exclaim as above.]

line See what I am taking.
drawing [The Midē' has pulled up a medicinal root. This denotes his possessing a wonderful medicine and appears in the order of an advertisement.]

line See me, whose head is out of water.
drawing

On Pl. XXII , B , is presented an illustration reproduced from a piece of birch bark owned by the preceptor of "Little Frenchman," of the import of which the latter was ignorant. His idea of the signification of the characters is based upon general information which he has received, and not upon any pertaining directly to the record. From general appearances the song seems to be a private 293 record pertaining to the Ghost Society, the means through which the recorder attained his first degree of the Midē'wiwin, as well as to his abilities, which appear to be boastfully referred to:

mnemonic song
Plate XXII.b. Mnemonic Song.

line I am sitting with my pipe.
drawing [Midē' sitting, holding his pipe. He has been called upon to visit a patient, and the filled pipe is handed to him to smoke preparatory to his commencing the ceremony of exorcism.]

line I employ the spirit, the spirit of the owl.
drawing [This evidently indicates the Owl Man'idō, which has been referred to in connection with the Red Lake Midē' chart, Pl. III , No. 113. The Owl man'idō is there represented as passing from the Midē'wigân to the Dzhibai' Midē'wigân, and the drawings in that record and in this are sufficiently alike to convey the idea that the maker of this song had obtained his suggestion from the old Midē' chart.]

line It stands, that which I am going after.
drawing [The Midē', impersonating the Bear Man'idō, is seeking a medicinal tree of which he has knowledge, and certain parts of which he employs in his profession. The two footprints indicate the direction the animal is taking.]

line I, who fly.
drawing [This is the outline of a Thunder bird, who appears to grasp in his talons some medical plants.]

line Ki'-bi-nan' pi-zan'. Ki'binan' is what I use, it flies like an arrow.
drawing [The Midē''s arm is seen grasping a magic arrow, to symbolize the velocity of action of the remedy.]

line I am coming to the earth.
drawing [A Man'idō is represented upon a circle, and in the act of descending toward the earth, which is indicated by the horizontal line, upon which is an Indian habitation. The character to denote the sky is usually drawn as a curved line with the convexity above, but in this instance the ends of the lines are continued below, so as to unite and to complete the ring; the intention being, as suggested by several Midē' priests, to denote great altitude above the earth, i.e., higher than the visible azure sky, which is designated by curved lines only.]

line I am feeling for it.
drawing [The Midē' is reaching into holes in the earth in search of hidden medicines.]

line I am talking to it.
drawing [The Midē' is communing with the medicine Man'idō' with the Midē' sack, which he holds in his hand. The voice lines extend from his mouth to the sack, which appears to be made of the skin of an Owl, as before noted in connection with the second character in this song.]

294 They are sitting round the interior or in a row.
line [This evidently signifies the Ghost Lodge, as the structure is drawn at right angles to that usu-

ally made to represent the Midē′wigân, and also because it seems to be reproduced from the Red Lake chart already alluded to and figured in Pl. III, No. 112. The spirits or shadows, as the dead are termed, are also indicated by crosses in like manner.]

line drawing: You who are newly hung; you have reached half, and you are now full.

[The allusion is to three phases of the moon, probably having reference to certain periods at which some important ceremonies or events are to occur.]

line drawing: I am going for my dish.

[The speaker intimates that he is going to make a feast, the dish being shown at the top in the form of a circle; the footprints are directed toward it and signify, by their shape, that he likens himself to the Bear man′idō, one of the guardians of the Midēwiwin.]

line drawing: I go through the medicine lodge.

[The footprints within the parallel lines denote his having passed through an unnamed number of degrees. Although the structure is indicated as being erected like the Ghost Lodge, i.e., north and south, it is stated that Midēwiwin is intended. This appears to be an instance of the non-systematic manner of objective ideagraphic delineation.]

line drawer: Let us commune with one another.

[The speaker is desirous of communing with his favorite man′idōs, with whom he considers himself on an equality, as is indicated by the anthropomorphic form of one between whom and himself the voice lines extend.]

On Figs. 36-39, are reproduced several series of pictographs from birch-bark songs found among the effects of a deceased Midē′ priest, at Leech Lake. Reference to other relics belonging to the same collection has been made in connection with effigies and beads employed by Midē′ in the endeavor to prove the genuineness of their religion and profession. These mnemonic songs were exhibited to many Midē′ priests from various portions of the Ojibwa country, in the hope of obtaining some satisfactory explanation regarding the import of the several characters; but, although they were pronounced to be "Grand Medicine," no suggestions were offered beyond the merest repetition of the name of the object or what it probably was meant to represent. The direction of their order was mentioned, because in most instances the initial character furnishes the guide. Apart from this, the illustrations are of interest as exhibiting the superior character and cleverness of their execution.

295

song as described in text

Fig. 36. —Leech Lake Midē′ song.

The initial character on Fig. 36 appears to be at the right hand upper corner, and represents the Bear Man′idō. The third figure is that of the Midē′wiwin, with four man′idōs within it, probably the guardians of the four degrees. The owner of the song was a Midē′ of the second degree, as was stated in connection with his Midē′wi-gwas or "medicine chart," illustrated on Plate III, C.

song as described in text

Fig. 37. —Leech Lake Midē′ song.

Fig. 37 represents what appears to be a mishkiki or medicine song, as is suggested by the figures of plants and roots. It is impossible to state absolutely at which side the initial character is placed, though it would appear that the human figure at the upper left hand corner would be more in accordance with the common custom.

song as described in text

Fig. 38. —Leech Lake Midē′ song.

Fig. 38 seems to pertain to hunting, and may have been recognized as a hunter's chart. According to the belief of several Midē′, it is lead from right to left, the human figure indicating the direction according to the way in which the heads of the crane, bear, etc., are turned. The lower left hand figure of a man has five marks upon the breast, which probably indicate mī′gis spots, to denote the power of magic influence possessed by the recorder.

296

song as described in text

Fig. 39. —Leech Lake Midē′ song.

The characters on Fig. 39 are found to be arranged so as to read from the right hand upper corner toward the left, the next line continuing to the right and lastly again to the left, terminating with the figure of a Midē′ with the mī′gis upon his breast. This is interesting on account of the boustrophic system of delineating the figures, and also because such instances are rarely found to occur.

298

DRESS AND ORNAMENTS.

While it is customary among many tribes of Indians to use as little clothing as possible when engaged in dancing, either of a social or ceremonial nature, the Ojibwa, on the contrary, vie with one another in the attempt to appear in the most costly and gaudy dress attainable. The Ojibwa Midē′ priests, take particular pride in their appearance when attending ceremonies of the Midē′ Society, and seldom fail to impress this fact upon visitors, as some of the Dakotan tribes, who have adopted similar medicine ceremonies after the custom of their Algonkian neighbors are frequently without any clothing other than the breechcloth and moccasins and the armlets and other attractive ornaments. This disregard of dress appears, to the Ojibwa, as a sacrilegious digression from the ancient usages, and it frequently excites severe comment.

Apart from facial ornamentation, of such design as may take the actor's fancy, or in accordance with the degree of which the subject may be a member, the Midē′ priests wear shirts, trousers, and moccasins, the first two of which may consist of flannel or cloth and be either plain or ornamented with beads, while the latter are always of buckskin, or, what is more highly prized, moose skin, beaded or worked with colored porcupine quills.

dancing garters
Plate XXIII. Midē´ Dancing Garters. Immediately below each knee is tied a necessary item of an Ojibwa's dress, a garter, which consists of a band of beads varying in different specimens from 2 to 4 inches in width, and from 18 to 20 inches in length, to each end of which strands of colored wool yarn, 2 feet long, are attached so as to admit of being passed around the leg and tied in a bow-knot in front. These garters are made by the women in such patterns as they may be able to design or elaborate. On Pl. XXIII are reproductions of parts of two patterns which are of more than ordinary interest, because of the symbolic signification of the colors and the primitive art design in one, and the substitution of colors and the introduction of modern designs in the other. The upper one consists of green, red, and white beads, the first two colors being in accord with those of one of the degree posts, while the white is symbolical of the mī´gis shell. In the lower illustration is found a substitution of color for the preceding, accounted for by the Midē´ informants, who explained that neither of the varieties of beads of the particular color desired could be obtained when wanted. The yellow beads are substituted for white, the blue for green, and the orange and pink for red. The design retains the lozenge form, though in a different arrangement, and the introduction of the blue border is adapted after patterns observed among their white neighbors. In the former is presented also what the Ojibwa term the groundwork or type of their original style of ornamentation, i.e., wavy or gently zigzag lines. Later art work consists 299 chiefly of curved lines, and this has gradually become modified through instruction from the Catholic sisters at various early mission establishments until now, when there has been brought about a common system of working upon cloth or velvet, in patterns, consisting of vines, leaves, and flowers, often exceedingly attractive though not aboriginal in the true sense of the word.

Bands of flannel or buckskin, handsomely beaded, are sometimes attached to the sides of the pantaloons, in imitation of an officer's stripes, and around the bottom. Collars are also used, in addition to necklaces of claws, shells, or other objects.

Armlets and bracelets are sometimes made of bands of beadwork, though brass wire or pieces of metal are preferred.

Bags made of cloth, beautifully ornamented or entirely covered with beads, are worn, supported at the side by means of a broad band or baldric passing over the opposite shoulder. The head is decorated with disks of metal and tufts of colored horse hair or moose hair and with eagle feathers to designate the particular exploits performed by the wearer.

Few emblems of personal valor or exploits are now worn, as many of the representatives of the present generation have never been actively engaged in war, so that there is generally found only among the older members the practice of wearing upon the head eagle feathers bearing indications of significant markings or cuttings. A feather which has been split from the tip toward the middle denotes that the wearer was wounded by an arrow. A red spot as large as a silver dime painted upon a feather shows the wearer to have been wounded by a bullet. The privilege of wearing a feather tipped with red flannel or horse hair dyed red is recognized only when the wearer has killed an enemy, and when a great number have been killed in war the so-called war bonnet is worn, and may consist of a number of feathers exceeding the number of persons killed, the idea to be expressed being "a great number," rather than a specific enumeration.

Although the Ojibwa admit that in former times they had many other specific ways of indicating various kinds of personal exploits, they now have little opportunity of gaining such distinction, and consequently the practice has fallen into desuetude.

FUTURE OF THE SOCIETY.

According to a treaty now being made between the United States Government and the Ojibwa Indians, the latter are to relinquish the several areas of land at present occupied by them and to remove to portions of the Red Lake and White Earth Reservations and take lands in severalty. By this treaty about 4,000,000 acres of land will be ceded to the Government, and the members of the various bands will become citizens of the United States, and thus their tribal ties 300 will be broken and their primitive customs and rites be abandoned.

The chief Midē´ priests, being aware of the momentous consequences of such a change in their habits, and foreseeing the impracticability of much longer continuing the ceremonies of so-called "pagan rites," became willing to impart them to me, in order that a complete description might be made and preserved for the future information of their descendants.

There is scarcely any doubt that these ceremonies will still be secretly held at irregular intervals; but under the watchful care of the national authorities it is doubtful whether they will be performed with any degree of completeness, and it will be but a comparatively short time before the Midē´wiwin will be only a tradition.

Footnotes
1. Coll. Minn. Hist. Soc., 1885, vol. 5, p. 130.
2. Reproduced from the ninth volume of the New York Colonial Documents, pp. 1054, 1055.
3. New Voyages to North America, London, 1703, vol. 2, pp. 47, 48.
4. London, 1689, p. 59, et seq.
5. Information respecting the history, condition, and prospects of the Indian tribes of the United States. Philadelphia, 1851, vol. 1, p. 319.
6. Ibid., p. 362.
7. Op. cit., vol. 5, p. 423.
8. Op. cit., pp. 65, 66.
9. Op. cit., vol. 5, p, 71.
10. Op. cit., p. 25.
11. History of the Ojebway Indians, London [1843(?)], pp. 143,144.
12. Op. cit., p. 78 et seq.
13. Op. cit., p. 81.
14. Vol. 1, No. 3, 1888, p. 216, Figs.

2 and 3.

15. History of the Ojebway Indians, etc., London (1843?), pp. 145, 146.

16. Hist. of the Ojebway Indians. London [1843?], p. 155.

Transcriber's Footnotes:

A.

The chief priest then says to him, "Ō´mishga‘n"—"get up"—which he does

The backward apostrophe in **Ō´mishga‘n** occurs nowhere else in the text; it may be phonetic (glottal stop?) or an error.

B.

Gi´-gi-min´-ĕ-go´-min mi-dē´-wi-wĭn mi-dē´ man´-i-dō´ 'n-gi-gĭn´-o-a-mâk

The apostrophe in **'n-gi-gĭn´-o-a-mâk** occurs nowhere else in the text; it may be phonetic (elision?) or an error.